Duty to Serve, Duty to Conscience

The Story of Two Conscientious Objector Combat Medics during the Vietnam War

James C. Kearney
and
William H. Clamurro

Number 21 in the North Texas Military Biography
and Memoir Series

University of North Texas Press
Denton, Texas

Permissions:
University of North Texas Press
1155 Union Circle #311336
Denton, TX 76203-5017

The paper used in this book meets the minimum requirements of the American National Standard for Permanence of Paper for Printed Library Materials, z39.48.1984. Binding materials have been chosen for durability.

Library of Congress Cataloging-in-Publication Data

Kearney, James C., 1946- author. | Clamurro, William H., author.
  Duty to serve, duty to conscience : the story of two conscientious objector combat medics during the Vietnam War / James C. Kearney and William H. Clamurro.
    Pages cm
  Includes bibliographical references and index.
  ISBN-13 978-1-57441-896-5 (cloth)
  ISBN-13 978-1-57441-903-0 (ebook)
  1. LCSH: Kearney, James C., 1946– 2. Clamurro, William H. 3. United States. Army—Medical personnel—Biography. 4. Vietnam War, 1961–1975—Medical care. 5. Vietnam War, 1961–1975—Conscientious objectors—United States—Biography. 6. Vietnam War, 1961–1975—Personal narratives, American. 7. BISAC: HISTORY / Wars & Conflicts / Vietnam War 8. BIOGRAPHY & AUTOBIOGRAPHY / Military 9. LCGFT: Autobiographies. 10. Personal narratives.

  DS559.44 .K43 2023
  959.704/3092 [B]–dc23
                        2023003601

Duty to Serve, Duty to Conscience is Number 21 in the North Texas Military Biography and Memoir Series.

The electronic edition of this book was made possible by the support of the Vick Family Foundation.

Typeset by vPrompt eServices.

For Bob Childress and
all our other classmates from basic training
who perished in Vietnam

Contents

Poems

by William Clamurro

Acknowledgments

Numerous people have helped the two of us in the writing of this book, contributing in many ways—from reading preliminary drafts of our texts to finding long-lost or forgotten materials and providing advice and encouragement. Briefly, we would like to acknowledge their contributions.

We are both indebted to Dr. Jean Mansavage and Gary Kulik, who peer reviewed the manuscript for the publisher. Both offered invaluable suggestions for revisions that improved both accuracy and readability. As a fellow 1-A-O Vietnam medic, Gary Kulik knew the story from the inside; as an author of a well-respected book on Vietnam himself, he also offered many stylistic and organizational suggestions. Dr. Mansavage's doctoral dissertation, "'A Sincere and Meaningful Belief': Legal Conscientious Objection during the Vietnam War" (Texas A&M University, College Station, Texas, 2000), provided us with indispensable facts and figures necessary for our work. Her dissertation is the only substantial and meticulously researched scholarly study on the subject known to us.

For Bill Clamurro significant help came from Henry Sayre and Amy Sage Webb-Baza in reading preliminary drafts. Herbert and Suzy Achleitner were instrumental, insisting that Bill retrieve and publish the thirty-two poems, lost and recovered from his time in Vietnam. Jack Hailey proved to be a crucial resource for Bill by finding more than thirty letters that Bill had mailed to him during this time.

Jim Kearney is especially indebted to the involvement of Ms. Evan Windham and others of the Bob Bullock Museum, University of Texas, Austin, for the making of the podcast that recounts the development of his decision to become a 1-A-O and his experiences in Vietnam, including the harrowing helicopter medevac mission during which he was wounded. He also wants to thank the crew members from that experience: Greg Simpson, US Army (retired), Doc Holiday, and David Weeks.

Finally, both of us want to acknowledge the input and interest of Andrew Phelan and Fred Ervin, fellow 1-A-O medics and colleagues during training at Fort Sam Houston. We also thank Carlos Alvarado, chief archivist at the Army Medical Museum at Fort Sam Houston, who took a personal interest in our project and offered valuable suggestions on more than one occasion.

All of these friends and colleagues contributed in many ways, and it should be said that our story, while mainly ours, represents a collaboration with others. Above all, this is a tribute to them and many others, unnamed, whose participation in the experiences in Vietnam and whose encouragement later have shaped this book.

Abbreviations

AC	aircraft commander
AIT	advanced individual training
AO	area of operation
APC	armored personnel carriers
ARVN	army of the Republic of Vietnam
CO	conscientious objector
COINTELPRO	Counterintelligence Program
COSVN	Central Office for South Vietnam
DEROS	date eligible for return from overseas
DI	drill instructor
EM	enlisted men
FSB	fire support base
GI	general issue (enlisted men)
IV	intravenous (solution)
MASH	mobile army surgical hospital
MEDCAP	medical civic outreach project
MOS	military occupational specialty
MP	military police
NCO	noncommissioned officer
NVA	North Vietnamese Army
PTSD	post-traumatic stress disorder
PX	army commissary (formerly "post exchange")
R&R	rest and recuperation
RA	regular army
ROTC	reserve officers' training corps
RPG	rocket-propelled grenade
RVN	Republic of Vietnam
SDS	Students for a Democratic Society

SSS	Selective Service System
STD	sexually transmitted disease
UT	University of Texas
VC	Viet Cong
WO	warrant officer

Prologue
(*Kearney*)

It was January 29, 1971. The place was Phuoc Vinh, about forty miles north-northeast of Saigon, where the headquarters of the 1st Air Cavalry Division had located. Medevac Command and Control had received a desperate call for help. An ambush by the North Vietnamese Army (NVA) in the jungle had led to a desperate, ongoing firefight that had resulted in casualties with life-threatening wounds. Medevac Command and Control scrambled to put a crew together. The medic was missing from the first-up crew and all the other medevac crews were out on missions. Although I had less than a week remaining on my tour of duty in Vietnam, I volunteered for the mission, as any of my fellow medics would have done under the circumstances. "So that others may live"—that was our motto and a mission statement that we all took seriously. In a matter of minutes our Huey, with its large red crosses and its ad hoc crew, was over the firefight. As we descended down the narrow hole in the triple canopy jungle, we spied a cluster of GIs (enlisted men) huddled behind a large tree trunk that had fallen flat, offering some cover. A GI with a sucking chest wound lay stretched out below us on the jungle floor. As we made our way down, slowly and cautiously, clipping limbs on either side, I swung out the hoist and prepared to throw out the special litter for nonambulatory patients. We all were tense, and the adrenalin was flowing. We had a phrase for it: the combat assault butterflies. The unmistakable chatter of machine-gun fire over the roar of the helicopter had announced even before our descent that it was going to be a "hot" hoist, the most dangerous situation for a medevac crew. We came to a hover about fifty feet above the huddled GIs. Kneeling in the open door, I threw out the special litter and with the handheld control began running out the cable to which the litter would be affixed.

Then all hell broke loose. The fierce firefight between the GIs crouched behind the log and the NVA hidden in the jungle erupted anew to break the brief pause that had allowed us to descend. Our gunner, David Kramer, opened up to join the fray and make it a three-way affair. The NVA obliged with a burst from their own machine gun, which sent a spray of bullets our way. Both Kramer and I were hit while the Huey took multiple rounds from one end of the fuselage to the other. Luckily, the durable machine stayed airborne. The aircraft commander, Warrant Officer Greg Simpson, aborted the mission and we were able to lift out of the hole and limp our way to the nearest aid station only a few kilometers distant. My wounds, though serious, were not life threatening. My friend Bill "Groucho" Clamurro was on duty at the aid station where we sat down. Bill administered first aid, a fitting conclusion and circularity to our improbable friendship and stint as combat medics—medics who also represented a new breed of conscientious objectors (COs)—namely, those whose opposition to war came about not "by reason of religious training and upbringing," as was the case for the great majority of our fellow 1-A-O medics, but as a result of a personal ethical journey and an informed political and historical awareness.

***

Despite all that has been written about Vietnam, the story of the individual, "political/ethical" 1-A-O medic has yet to be told. Our experience of the draft, of the Vietnam War, and even of the postwar reckoning differed fundamentally from that of the great majority of our fellow draftees and even from our fellow 1-A-Os whose opposition to weapons was entirely faith based. This was brought home to me forcibly with the publication of a new book by Ron Donahey, *Vietnam Combat Medic: A Conscientious Objector in the Central Highlands*, (Atlanta: Deeds Publishing, 2018). My (used) copy of the book includes an inscription by the author that is telling:

If it were not for the protection given to me by my Savior Jesus Christ, this story would never be told—Ron

His absolute faith is inspirational, but the experience of Bill Clamurro and myself, and those like us, filtered through an entirely different sensibility. By and large we were older, more highly educated, and better informed, both historically and politically. And I mention the last characteristic not out of snobbery but as a simple fact. Although most of us had experienced some degree of religious training from our parents and church, neither organized religion nor an intense personal faith stood in the forefront of our decision to apply for 1-A-O CO status.

Our inspiration came from an entirely different source—broadly speaking, from the Humanist tradition in Western civilization and, more specifically, from that intellectual revolution known as the Enlightenment, a movement that had given rise to, among other things, the Constitution of the United States that we were sworn to defend. We had embraced these attitudes and they sustained us daily. Our day-to-day experiences validated at every turn what we already had come to believe before we entered military service, and this fact sets the present narrative apart in a fundamental way from much of what has been written about Vietnam.

Also, for us the war was existential, random, arbitrary. We existed day in and day out during our tours of duty under a cloud of uncertainty and with an ever-present cynicism; whether we survived or not had nothing to do with divine intervention but rather was almost entirely a matter of the luck of the draw or the toss of the dice, and if we were killed or wounded, it would be just another small addition to the monumental waste that we encountered at every turn. We also shared the conviction that informed and responsible dissent, which our special status embodied, was a higher form of patriotism than passive, uncritical acquiescence to the official line propagated by our leaders at the highest level. Was that not a bedrock principle of our democracy and hence a civic duty incumbent upon us? We believed so.

And yet we performed our duties as medics, often as frontline medics, apolitically and professionally almost to a man—a seeming contradiction. To my knowledge there were no instances of gross dereliction of duty or seditious activity. Newspaper articles of the period routinely lauded the courage of the 1-A-O medics in Vietnam. The spreading discontent within the ranks of the army during the latter phases of the war, especially among the draftees, that began to eat at unit cohesion and battle readiness surprisingly, almost counterintuitively, found little support among us. How could this be? Perhaps our story will cast a fresh light on an apparent paradox: we were not just COs but first and foremost conscientious medics.

The army, however, viewed the appearance of this new breed of political rather than religious objector with grave suspicion. It was an appearance unique to the Vietnam War and perhaps unique to warfare in general. We are convinced this suspicion, even alarm, that spread from the army to the highest echelons of the Selective Service System (SSS), and thence to Capitol Hill, contributed significantly to the termination of the draft in 1973—an interpretation that, if valid, casts the demise of the draft in a whole new light. Be that as it may, our stories should help to allay those concerns, on the one hand, even as it sheds new light on the debate about the draft, its termination, and its possible reintroduction on the other.

Our story is also is the story of a friendship that began in 1969 and continues to the present. Bill Clamurro and I met at Fort Sam Houston in the summer of 1969, where we took both basic training and advanced individual training (AIT) to become army medics. We had both recently graduated from college, at which point we had been reclassified 1-A, eligible for the draft. Vietnam was on everyone's mind then, especially if you were close to graduation. The game-changing Tet Offensive had dominated the headlines for most of 1968, bringing the reality of the war into the living rooms of most Americans. US troop numbers had peaked that year at 549,500. Student protests and unrest also filled the evening news. The draft, which supported the large American force abroad, had become a lightning rod for student dissent at home and a preoccupation for those approaching graduation, at which point, as with us, their student deferments ended. Certainly, for Bill and me, as well as for millions of others, the draft was an inseparable part of the

Vietnam experience, and so this, as well as our growing political and moral engagement, forms an important part of our story.

By graduation we had both become firmly opposed to the war, albeit following very different paths. What to do? It was a dilemma that we shared with many thousands of our generation. Faced with involuntary participation in a war that we had come to detest, each had to decide for himself: Did duty to country mandate service, even in a bad cause, or was it a higher duty to resist, to evade, or even to desert, and by so doing to become, as many deserters and draft evaders did, a man without a country, often even rejected by one's own family and friends? It was a very personal decision for which there was no right or wrong answer. Everyone had to confront the situation and decide for himself. The extraordinary number of draftees faced with this dilemma became one of the defining factors that separated Vietnam from other wars of the twentieth century.

The answer for both Bill and me was a compromise. We decided that we would be willing to put on the uniform and serve if we could do so as noncombatants; indeed, we were both motivated by a strong sense of duty to country, as the title to this book suggests. We discovered that the Selective Service law actually provided for this scenario by permitting two types of COs: those willing to put on a uniform (1-A-Os)—always a distinct minority—and those only accepting alternative service outside the military (1-Os). In both cases, however, one's reason for application had to be "by reason of religious training and belief" and, moreover, one had to be opposed to "war in any form," not just the war at hand.[1] This presented certain quandaries that are dealt with at length in our respective narratives, but for the present, as we look back, we are both surprised by how uninformed we actually were about the broader significance of our status. At the time the 1-A-O classification, if granted, appeared as an immediate solution to our common dilemma—compulsory service in a war we opposed—and we both took advantage of it. Only later, in the course of researching and writing this book, did the full significance of the 1-A-O classification begin to sink in, both as an overlooked story in Vietnam and as a central chapter in the broader history of pacifism in this country. With this growing awareness that we had participated in something quite extraordinary, our purpose and focus began to shift. Our own narratives should serve the larger purpose of enhancing appreciation for the 1-A-O story and, especially, for our particular subchapter of that story—those more political than religious in their convictions. In line with this wider purpose, our book also includes thought essays at the end of the narrative that reflect on the significance of the classification and also on the loss to the country that occurred when the classification ended with the termination of the draft in 1973.

Looking back, we were right in opposing the war. We have a quiet pride in having taken a stand and acted in accordance with our consciences. But self-righteousness is not our story. Many believed our government and thought the cause was noble. Others felt strongly that it was their patriotic duty to serve, even if in a bad cause. We respect these points of view. Everyone had to decide for himself, and the degree to which this happened was unique to Vietnam and goes a long way to explaining the war's continued fascination. Our response—the decision to serve as medics in a war we felt strongly was wrong, but only under the condition that we receive no weapons training and that we could not be compelled to carry or use weapons—also deserves to be told.

It is our sincere hope that the resulting effort will not only mark and celebrate our fifty-plus years of friendship— a friendship that began at Fort Sam Houston, strengthened in Vietnam, and continued to grow and mature over the intervening years—but will also contribute to the memory of the extraordinary story of 1-A-O medics in Vietnam, and particularly those who were more political than religious in their opposition. We existed, after all, and our story deserves a seat at the table.

Chapter 1

Texas A&M

"Pray for War," or
"Dulce bellum inexpertis"

(*Kearney*)

How did I become a 1-A-O CO, the only person to ever apply for and receive such status from the rural county in Texas where I grew up? A deep-seated skepticism lingers about those like me who applied for the classifications during the Vietnam War, especially for those who were more political than religious in their leanings, and where the charge of "expediency" rather than "sincere conviction" was often leveled. Even as we relate our personal stories, our narratives should help to set the record straight about the 1-A-O status, for checking this box on the application form SSS 150 was anything other than an easy out; indeed, the classification, if granted by one's local draft board, often resulted in combat duty.

For my part there was little tradition of military service in my family, but neither was there an atmosphere of hostility toward the military. My own father had been too young for World War I and too old for World War II. Once, sometime in the 1920s, he had completed a month-long stint at Fort Sam Houston in San Antonio in what was then called the Citizens' Military Training Camps.[1] The program, largely forgotten now, aimed to give young men of military age in the period between the wars a modicum of military training without any obligation to serve on active duty.

My father's brief exposure to military life at Fort Sam Houston is meaningful to me because that is also where I began and ended my army career. He had been enrolled in a cavalry unit and often told a very humorous story about his abbreviated military career. At the end of the prescribed training, a grand review was ordered to show off the freshly minted citizen soldiers at the parade grounds of Fort Sam Houston in San Antonio. Just as my father and his unit rode past the assembled brass with swords drawn, a cannon was discharged. My father's horse spooked, and the terrified beast bolted headlong into the crowd of dignitaries, scattering them like sheep. The last thing anyone saw was the frightened horse, my father still astride with saber drawn, a half a mile away at a full run in the opposite direction. This little episode marked the highlight of his abbreviated military career.

My abrupt initiation into military life was more accident than design, a by-product of certain class dynamics that channeled me and my brother toward Texas A&M at College Station, then a backwater on the Brazos River in Central Texas. I was a country boy—my father a rancher, my formative years spent on the family ranch—and I comported willingly to what was expected of a rancher's son. At that time the sons and daughters of ranchers and farmers attended land-grant colleges, like Texas A&M, or junior colleges, or so-called teachers' colleges. To do otherwise would raise eyebrows.

At the time Texas A&M had about five thousand undergraduates and was lone among the larger state institutions of higher education in Texas to require undergraduate membership in the corps of cadets (ROTC, or reserve officers' training corps) and to restrict undergraduate admission to males. This imparted a distinct flavor that generations of Aggies cherished and faithfully upheld. It also led many alumni to fiercely resist any attempt to bring the school more in line with the times. But, alas, change is inevitable, and these changes have transformed the university over time into something that bears faint resemblance to the school I attended. Today it is a megauniversity of sixty thousand–plus students, 47 percent of whom are female. Only 4 percent (or 2,300) out of this total now belong to the corps of cadets. Still, an unmistakable institutional nostalgia for the Old Army days lingers and very much colors the school's culture even to the present.

In the 1960s the school was still genuinely Old Army, or Brown Belt Army, as with Gen. Pershing in World War I. The school even perpetuated certain terms and phrases that clearly dated back to World War I, such as "to take gas" when things go really wrong. I find myself unconsciously still using the phrase now and then only to evince perplexed looks from those within earshot. They know "to pass gas," but to "take gas" doesn't compute. Broadly speaking, the term *Old Army* suggested a no-nonsense attitude of mental and physical toughness, while in practical terms it meant an intricate system of privileges based on class standing and was enforced by an extreme, indeed brutal, regimen of physical and mental hazing that had evolved over the decades since the school first opened its doors for business in 1876 as a land-grant college. The physical hazing continued to be tolerated by the school administration long after such practices had been abandoned elsewhere and was still very much part of the A&M culture when I was there in 1964–65.

This was, of course, a conscious policy, part and parcel of being Old Army, and, I suppose, a general attitude followed by most military schools everywhere to one degree or another, all based on the supposition that in order to construct a good soldier, you must first thoroughly deconstruct him both psychologically and physically so that he becomes an unquestioning herd animal that will even follow the herd over the cliff if need be. My problem was that I was always the one animal who stood back and said, "Wait a minute, let's think about this. Do we really want to run over a cliff?"

It was this sense of trial by fire that forged such fierce loyalties on the part of those who made it through to their senior year, allowing them to wear the coveted brown riding boots, cinch up

Animal A, Texas A&M, 1964–65.

the distinctive Sam Browne belts, don the World War I–era felt campaign hats, and, upon graduation, place the oversized Aggie rings upon their fingers with which to proudly mark their tribal identity for the rest of their lives.

> Good bye to Texas University
> So long to the orange and the white
> Good luck to dear old Texas Aggies
> They are the boys who show the real old fight[2]

I survived my freshman year, and this in itself was an accomplishment since nearly half of the freshmen in my outfit, Animal A, had dropped out by this point either because they could not stomach the continual hazing or because their grades had deteriorated to the point that withdrawal was preferable to Fs on their permanent record. But as graduation approached, my discontent unexpectedly increased rather than waned even as the hazing eased up. The heretical notion took hold in me that this whole system was incompatible with the idea of higher education—and by far the majority of students were there, after all, to earn a degree and not to prepare for a military career—so I found it odd how few people seemed to share this insight. Even though I successfully made it through my freshman year and passed all of my classes, thereby earning the right to inflict compensatory torment on freshmen the coming year, I decided to forego this reward and part ways with the Texas A&M Corps of Cadets.

The first winds of change arrived at the school that year. Beginning with the fall semester of 1965, it became possible to be an undergraduate at A&M while not a member of the corps of cadets. I had decided that a profession in the liberal arts was more to my liking than a career in engineering or agriculture, the calling cards of A&M. Moreover, I wanted to focus on my studies free from the distractions of the corps, its expectations being too all-consuming, with only a very few students having the wherewithal to excel at both. When it came time for the final review, I did not join my classmates for the symbolic final march that marked passage from freshman to sophomore status—the only one in my outfit to do so.

As I look back, the frustrations I had experienced in my studies that first year, rather than any deep-seated aversion to military life, was my main motivation for this decision. The following academic year, 1965–66, was probably the unhappiest year of my life for reasons that are not all that clear to me even to this day. But as I look back, I think it was largely (and simply) a matter of sexual frustration. I was a normal guy with a well-developed libido, but I had no meaningful relationships with the opposite gender, and A&M, still all male, was definitely not a fertile ground in this regard. This frustration, plus the growing realization that Texas A&M was not the best school at which to pursue a degree in the liberal arts, led to my decision to transfer to the University of Texas (UT) the following year (1965–66), becoming no doubt a traitor in the eyes of many of my classmates, who regarded the University of Texas as irredeemably decadent. But I was also emerging as a growing enigma to my parents, who neither understood nor applauded the change even as they expressed a quiet pride in my academic accomplishments.

As I look back, however, the A&M experience was not all bad, and I often find myself looking upon it with nostalgia. It offered interesting insight into human behavior in extreme situations: those who suffered the most as freshmen became, almost invariably, the harshest and least sympathetic when it came their turn to dish it out. Once experienced, humiliation does not seem to reinforce compassion for most people; on the contrary, when the tables turn, the desire for compensatory gratification usually drowns out kinder impulses. This was a revelation to me. The role of elemental tribalism in human affairs was also eye-opening. Humans need to belong. I voluntarily chose to renounce my position in the tribe and become a solitary pilgrim, to my own emotional detriment, but when I hear the Aggie war hymn, something primal still stirs within me, and I realize that deep down I also share the impulse to belong.

But more importantly Texas A&M prepared me for subsequent entry into the real army when the time came. Being well versed in all military formalities and expectations, like saluting and showing proper deference to one's superiors, made the transition to the real army easier for me than most of my classmates in basic training for whom military life was a rude shock, both physically and mentally. Finally, I should say, it is necessary to comprehend both the attractions and deficiencies of the military mindset in order to grasp the flow of history, and A&M, as much as the real army, opened insights into both of these. Wars and warfare, sadly, have been a constant companion in human history, and the military is an important component in nearly all societies. I have never denied that a competent and well-trained military is necessary. It just wasn't for me.

During my years at Texas A&M, I was not politically engaged in any meaningful way. Our growing involvement in Southeast Asia was hardly ever mentioned, and I could not have told you where Vietnam was had my life depended on it. This is quite odd in retrospect, because every morning the whole corps of cadets, five thousand strong, gathered in the bottom floors of their respective dorms—twelve dorms in total that all faced a central courtyard—and at precisely 7:00 a.m. burst out of the dorms as one (it was called "falling out") all waving arms wildly and yelling in unison, "Pray for war, pray for war," the cry of thousands of voices reverberating across the whole campus. The cadets thereafter fell into formation and then marched, company by company, to the cavernous Sibesa Dining Hall, scarcely aware that very shortly for many among their ranks their prayers would be answered. Erasmus had put it succinctly: "Dulce bellum inexpertis!" (War is sweet for those with no experience of it!)

In the summer of 1966, between A&M and the University of Texas, an old hometown buddy and I decided to take a cheap flight (Icelandic) to Europe, where we were told we would be able to find employment for the summer, which we both succeeded in doing, he as a summer intern in a bank in Geneva and I on a construction job in southern Germany. We both stayed with our jobs for the first half of the summer, after which we rendezvoused in Geneva and from there made our way by train, bus, and thumb across Switzerland, France, England, and Scotland. We stayed in youth hostels when available and, if not, laid out our bedrolls in parks or other public places— quite an adventure for two rural country boys from Texas who had scarcely ventured out of our home state prior to this trip.

Our summer in Europe also offered a rude introduction to the Vietnam War and to anti-American sentiment, which was already widespread on the continent by that point and which I had never before experienced firsthand. But that summer was also noteworthy for another reason: the infamous tower shooting on the campus of the University of Texas on August 1, 1966, by erstwhile marine and Eagle Scout gone berserk Charles Whitman, the deadliest mass shooting in the United States up to that time. It was a shocking event, and for us embarrassing, for on more than one occasion we were confronted about being Texans and asked to explain how such a thing could take place. We could, of course, offer no explanation.

With this horrific event still fresh in the memory of students and faculty, the ending of an era of innocence, it seemed, I began my studies at the University of Texas in the fall of 1966. It was a much better fit for me. I longed for a more stimulating intellectual environment and, by and large, was not disappointed. I declared myself a history major and pretty much lived the life of a hermit that first six months, with very little in the way of a social life, although that began to improve as I gradually found my bearings and moved out of a house occupied by electrical engineering majors and into a co-ed dormitory, the so-called German House, which had just opened its doors and offered both room and board in two old refurbished houses conveniently located a couple of blocks west of the university.

The German House was a stimulating place. The inhabitants were not restricted to German majors by any means, the only criteria being an interest in the German language, which I had chosen for my language requirement, and a willingness to try to speak the language during mealtimes. The German House also hosted male and female exchange students from Germany each semester, and I had the opportunity to room with the first male exchange student, Christoph, in the spring of 1967. Besides being of different nationalities, we came from completely different backgrounds: he the scion of a distinguished German publishing family, I the product of rural Texas. It was a situation that easily could have turned awkward but instead became enriching to both and was the beginning of a lifelong friendship.

But most importantly for me at the time, the German House was co-ed. Finally, after the emotional barrenness of the all-male Texas A&M campus and the single-minded dedication of monkish electrical engineer majors with whom I roomed my first semester at UT, I now experienced a meaningful social life that included daily interactions with members of the opposite sex—and what a collection of intelligent, attractive, and liberated ladies had found their way to the German House. My spirits began to improve on all fronts.

I enjoyed my studies and began to venture far afield in my readings. I stumbled on the writings of the eccentric and brilliant English philosopher Lord Bertrand Russell, who was very much in the news those days because of his outspoken views on nuclear disarmament and, subsequently, the Vietnam War. The first book I read was *Has Man a Future?*[3] This little book, published originally in 1961, had a profound influence on me and awakened my political consciousness with a start. My path to CO, it is safe to say, began with Bertrand Russell and his fear that the Cold War arm's race between Russia and the West, unless somehow reined in, would lead inexorably to a nuclear holocaust that could destroy human civilization forever. I recognized clearly the mentality that could glibly rationalize employing weapons of mass destruction, for it was a tribal mindset not unlike what I had experienced firsthand in the corps of cadets at Texas A&M. Lord Russell so influenced me that I bought and devoured nearly all his other books that were not strictly philosophical or mathematical in nature, and this amounted to quite a pile in itself.

Bertrand Russell also helped me to awaken to the importance of nationalism in the modern world, about which he had written in his little book *Freedom and Organization*, 1814–1914.[4] This awareness received a further boost in the spring of 1967 when I was able to audit a graduate seminar given by a renowned international scholar and visiting professor, Dr. Hans Kohn, who at the time was recognized as perhaps the foremost scholar on the subject of nationalism by virtue of his massive study *The Idea of Nationalism*.[5]

In the meantime I was growing more aware of the Vietnam War by the day and was beginning to connect the dots: Vietnam ... colonialism ... nationalism, not Vietnam ... communism ... domino theory. I commenced, as many of my fellow students did, to gather every evening in the Chuck Wagon, the large student union at the University of Texas, to sip innumerable cups of coffee and to follow the CBS evening news with father Walter Cronkite. Vietnam, as has often been noted, was the first televised war, and we sat there glued to the screen, mesmerized by the images that were only a day or two removed from the actual battlefield.

My undergraduate years at the University of Texas coincided closely with the first stirrings of organized antiwar sentiment on the campus of UT. This unrest grew exponentially, so much so that by the time I became eligible for the draft after graduation in January of 1969, the University of Texas had clearly emerged as ground zero for student activism and antiwar sentiment in Texas,[6] much to the chagrin of the very conservative board of regents and its titular head, the strong-willed and controversial Frank Erwin. Erwin hated hippies, and everything else associated with student activism, with a primal passion. I can clearly remember seeing him driving down the Drag (the street fronting the western edge of the UT campus) in his orange and white Cadillac (UT colors), no doubt slightly inebriated—it was legal to drink and drive in Texas back then, and Erwin was a notorious lush—holding his hand and middle finger out the window in a well-known gesture of vulgarity directed at the hippies across the street from the university.

In the early spring of 1964, a small chapter of the Students for a Democratic Society (SDS) had organized on campus a scant four years after the first organizational meeting held in 1960 on the campus of the University of Michigan at Ann Arbor. Thereafter, the SDS expanded its membership exponentially on campuses across the country. It was the most important student organization to oppose the Vietnam War. From its embryonic beginnings, the UT chapter grew steadily in influence and numbers, and it is safe to say that the radicalization of the overwhelmingly white and conservative UT student body began with their efforts. In the fall of 1965, the local SDS organized the first antiwar protest: a death march around campus. About seventy students participated in the march and rally. It was also the first demonstration against the draft—an important development because on the college campuses across the country, opposition to the Vietnam War was inextricably linked to opposition to the draft.

The student newspaper, *The Daily Texan*, supported the protest on its editorial page and criticized the killings of Vietnamese children, whereupon an infuriated Frank Erwin threatened to abolish the *Daily Texan* editorial page. Following his lead, the board of regents began a full-scale assault on freedom of speech on the campus, intimidating students, faculty, and the editorial staff of the *Daily Texan* with a series of directives designed to throttle any criticism of the war or the establishment that promoted it. This development, in turn, encouraged student activists to organize an underground paper, *The Rag*, as a radical alternative to both the student newspaper, which began to echo the official line, and the mainstream media.

The Rag was one of the first and most important radical student papers of its kind in the nation and became a popular advocate for progressive thought of all stripes.[7] The paper also became the wellhead for the counterculture movement beginning to take shape in Austin that eventually blossomed to leave a rich artistic and musical, as well as political, legacy. Austin now advertises itself as the Live Music Capital of the World, and the annual South by Southwest festival has become an international happening that brings hundreds of thousands of visitors to the city every spring and infuses countless millions of dollars into the local economy. But how many remember its roots and reflect upon the irony inherent in this?

> Come gather 'round people
> Wherever you roam
> And admit that the waters
> Around you have grown[8]

Excitement was in the air back then and the new music legitimized it. It affected everyone and was a clarion call to either join or oppose. To me, at least initially, it was not so much antiwar as it was fresh versus stale, youthful vitality versus bloodless conformity that seemed to be choking us down at every turn. There was definitely a sexual component to it as well, with the youthful rebellion against the suffocating conventionality of the older generation. This new attitude

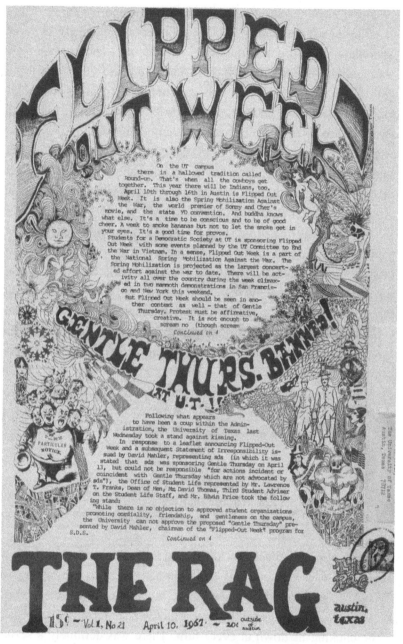

"Gentle Thursday Banned at UT," *The Rag*, April 10, 1967,
(camh-dob-012160), courtesy of The Dolph Briscoe Center for American
History, The University of Texas at Austin.

was very much enabled by the recent availability of the pill. Drugs, especially marijuana, were also in the mix, but this is something that I always steered clear of, then as now.

A new day seemed very much in the air, and it all came together in the event promoted by *The Rag* and the SDS called Gentle Thursday. It was organized "as a celebration of the belief that there is nothing wrong with fun."[9] It was wildly successful, with hundreds of students and area residents bringing kids, dogs, balloons, picnic lunches, and musical instruments to the West Mall of the University of Texas, beginning a years-long tradition and inspiring similar events at campuses around the country.

Naturally, the powers that be at the university took a dim view of this and summarily banned the second Gentle Thursday in Spring 1967, which, of course, had the effect of guaranteeing an even larger turnout

Gentle Thursday event in the spring of 1967. From the UT Traffic and Security Services Chief Allen R. Hamilton records (camh-dob-012158), courtesy of The Dolph Briscoe Center for American History, The University of Texas at Austin.

Spontaneous antiwar demonstration on the UT campus, May 6, 1970, in response to the Kent State shootings of May 4, 1970. From the George Carlson papers (camh-dob-012159), courtesy of The Dolph Briscoe Center for American History, The University of Texas at Austin.

when the organizers shifted the event to a nearby off-campus park. It was part of Flipped-Out Week, organized by SDS and *The Rag* in conjunction with the first national mobilization against the War in Vietnam. It included appearances on campus by SNCC (the Student Nonviolent Coordinating Committee) leader Stokely Carmichael, beat poet Allen Ginsberg, and Indian musician and guru Ravi Shankar. The SDS also organized antiwar protests at the nearby state capitol, during a visit by Vice President Hubert Humphrey, that turned into a police riot when the police waded into the crowd with their batons and handcuffs after firing tear gas. Six students were eventually charged and convicted of disorderly conduct and subsequently expelled from the university on the grounds that they had not shown proper respect for established authority.

My German roommate also nudged me in the direction of increased activism. Christoph was better informed and more politically engaged than I, and he took a keen interest in student protests at the University of Texas. Through him I gained a different perspective on my country, one that blended admiration with criticism born of frustration. Christoph was articulate, informed, and passionate, the sort of person who leaves a strong impression on nearly everyone he comes into contact with. Without a doubt he stimulated my growing political consciousness.

Thereafter I attended many protests, but I never officially joined the SDS or any other radical organization, for that matter. Oddly enough, even as my doubts about Vietnam grew, my instinctive distrust of herd mentality also revived, but this time prompted not so much by the authorities as by the demonstrators themselves. The large demonstration against Vice President Humphrey's visit to Austin in 1967 offered a case in point. It was certainly true that the police had gone on a rampage, which I witnessed firsthand, but there were also many members among the demonstrators who had deliberately provoked them and who seemed to be present more for the excitement than the cause itself. This had bothered me deeply and fostered a reluctance to fully commit to any single organization, even as my personal conviction that the war was fundamentally flawed was growing by leaps and bounds.

Two books helped to cement my conviction: Edwin Reischauer's *Beyond Vietnam: The United States and Asia*, and J. William Fulbright's *The Arrogance of Power*.[10] There have been many books written about Vietnam but as far as I am concerned, none are better than these two. Two distinguished public servants who also happened to be distinguished scholars endeavored in vain to redirect the national policy in respect to Southeast Asia, which, it seemed, had taken the wrong turn at every significant crossroad. Years later former secretary of defense Robert McNamara stated in his mea culpa, *Fog of War*, "If someone had just opened a book."[11] These were the books that should have been opened but were not. I am proud in retrospect that I did open both, and they affected me deeply.

Armadillo World Headquarters (poster by Jim Franklin).

And so 1968, my last undergraduate year at UT, rolled around. The protests continued almost on a daily basis; the counterculture in Austin continued to blossom, producing an amazingly rich cultural legacy that embraced art, theater, and music, and expanded to include other issues such as environmental activism, women's lib, and Chicano rights. Jim Franklin, the brilliant poster artist who provided many of the covers for *The Rag*, elevated the lowly armadillo as the symbol for this cultural awakening. Later, in 1973, Gary P. Nunn picked up on the idea with his "London Homesick Blues," and "Goin' Home to the Armadillo," the song that has endured as the theme song of the popular Austin City Limits.

The musical scene was particularly in ferment back then, producing various fusions of blues, rock, and country that eventually came to be known as redneck rock. I am happy to say that I attended concerts at three of the now-legendary venues of the period: Vulcan Gas Co., Armadillo World Headquarters, and Antone's blues club. These were the venues to showcase the interesting fusions that were beginning to take shape. Texas has such rich musical traditions from Chicano music to German and Czech polka bands, from the blues to hillbilly music, from gospel to Texas swing, and it all seemed to come together in Austin. But for the period, and in the context of the Vietnam War, one Texas product stands out, and that was Janice Joplin, the homely, eccentric white girl from Port Arthur, Texas, who could belt out the blues with the best of them, and who floated in and out of the Austin music scene, even briefly enrolling as a student at UT. She lived the new liberated life of drugs, sex, and excess to the hilt until it finally killed her.

My preoccupation with Vietnam, as was the case with many of my schoolmates, gathered steam as graduation approached because graduation meant losing the coveted II-S classification (student deferment) and being reclassified 1-A (eligible for the draft). And the closer this date approached, the more anxious I became. I had been in denial up until a month or so before graduation and had even made application and received acceptance to graduate school as a history major, as if the draft were a bad dream from which I would soon awake to blissfully continue my student existence in the isolated bubble of academia. With graduation scheduled for January of 1969, I began frantically searching about for escape routes.

> And it's one, two, three,
> What are we fighting for?
> Don't ask me, I don't give a damn,
> Next stop is Vietnam[12]

Prolongation by whatever means possible was a common strategy of the period, especially after the shock of the Tet Offensive in 1968. The NVA and Viet Cong (VC) launched surprise attacks across South Vietnam beginning January 30, 1968, during the traditional Tet New Year holidays, and continuing for six months or so thereafter. The NVA and the VC had counted on a spontaneous uprising among the South Vietnamese population, but this did not happen. Nevertheless, the scale, ferocity, and determination displayed by the enemy shocked the American public and underscored the disconnect between the US military's overly optimistic rhetoric about the war and the reality on the ground.

It is commonplace now to say that the Tet Offensive was a military disaster of the first order, but also a political victory that changed the whole narrative of the war and paved the way for ultimate victory of the NVA. Whether true or not, from my perspective at the time, Tet was definitely an eye-opener. It thrust the war front and center, gave the lie to all the glib rationalizations and delusional optimism of our military and political leaders, and, for the first time, placed the gore and horrors of war in the living rooms of America. And for those of us soon to be uprooted from our comfortable student existence and cast into the maelstrom, it was a wake-up call. The war was real.

I now stood at the threshold. I graduated in January of 1969 with a double major in history and German literature. As a means of prolonging my academic career through graduate school and forestalling the inevitable, I came up with the idea of enrolling in the ROTC program at UT, which says a lot about the confused state of my thinking at that moment in time. My convictions, neither politically nor ethically, had yet to coalesce into anything resembling coherence. Belatedly, I applied and was accepted to the ROTC program, and I notified my local draft board of the same. Obligingly, the board reclassified me 1-D, the category given to members of a reserve component, the National Guard, or students taking military training. This gave me breathing room, preventing my immediate reclassification to "eligible for the draft" and allowing me to begin my studies as a graduate student in the spring semester of 1969.

Vietnam was not my only preoccupation at the time by a long shot. During the course of 1968, I had become particularly interested in one very special woman who also resided at the German House, and this interest had increased gradually to the point that I imagined myself in love—madly in love, as a matter of fact. This was a problem, because although at times she seemed very encouraging, she was struggling with her own demons. It was an emotional roller coaster: one day she was warm and hopeful, the next day she came across as inexplicably cold and distant, but in the end, she was not able to reciprocate my feelings. And for me there was the maddening realization that because of my preoccupation with the draft, there was no way to compete on an even field. It finally came to a head in the winter of 1968–69, an unfortunate but not uncommon theme: romantic awakening against the backdrop of war. As I look back, the sadness of this outcome colored my whole Vietnam experience and influenced decisions on more than one occasion that in retrospect could only be considered foolhardy.

Things began to fall apart; my emotions in turmoil, I found it impossible to take my studies seriously. I began to fall seriously behind and eventually dropped all my classes, which, in turn, triggered reclassification by my draft board. Soon thereafter, on March 5, 1969, I received my summons—"Greetings, you are hereby …"—ordering me to report for a preinduction physical at the Federal Building in Houston, Texas, on April 3.

I was indeed a very alienated and unhappy young man during this period of my life. Nevertheless, I dutifully reported for the physical examination, which I passed. But in the course of the examination, all the inductees were asked to look over a list of organizations that were considered "hostile toward the American way of life" and to indicate affiliation, if any (see the Witness Statement, appendix 1). At the last moment the officer in charge added that we should also consider the SDS to be one of these subversive organizations, even though it was not on the list.

The question was relevant because a scant two weeks before, at the end of March 1969, the SDS had held its national convention in Austin.[13] The University of Texas, as expected, barred it from campus, but the Catholic Student Center across the street from the university opened its doors for the convention. It turned out to be an extremely contentious affair with the radical Spartacists attempting to oust the moderate wing and take over control of the organization. They failed, as it turned out, but it led to a schism from which the organization never fully recovered. That didn't really concern me, but what happened thereafter did.

Out of curiosity, and never with any serious intention of joining the organization, I paid five dollars and registered as a guest. I attended several lectures, including the plenum session, and was impressed with the high level of intelligence and sincere devotion to the cause on the part of many individual members. I realized, however, that I could never become an active member of the organization, because as I wrote in my journal, "They are an organization altogether too radical so that when one joins he must either accept their views hook, line, and sinker, or get out." My old antipathy toward herd mentality had kicked in once again. Nevertheless, I availed myself of the free literature being handed out by various groups that had set up booths. One of these booths passed out free copies of the writings of Chairman Mao Zedong, including the infamous Little Red Book. Mao's Cultural Revolution, it should be remembered, was in full swing at the time and very much in the news. Being curious, I took advantage of the free offer, filling my bag with several red-jacketed books by the venerable Chairman Mao, which I still possess.

This led to an interesting exchange, because a man near the booth followed me back to the German House, which was only a block removed from the church, and attempted to engage me in conversation and query me about my political beliefs. I was pretty naive at the time about this sort of thing, but not so much that I did not sense there was something very fishy about the man. He did not really look like a student, although he was obviously trying to pass himself off as one. Something about his bearing and demeanor gave it away and I began to suspect, correctly, as time would tell, that he was some sort of undercover agent fishing for dirt. I felt I had nothing to hide, but his creepiness put me off and I told him I was really not interested in discussing my political beliefs with a stranger. Very few people at the time had any inkling of how deeply paranoid the government was about student unrest and the civil rights movement and to what extreme lengths the government was willing to go to discredit both. Only much later, as the revelations concerning the FBI's secret Counterintelligence Program (COINTELPRO)[14] program began to surface, did I match up my own little encounter with this general paranoia, which, as we now know, went well beyond surveillance and dirty tricks to even include, very likely, assassinations.

Interestingly, the Austin Police Department, taking its cue from the FBI's COINTELPRO,[15] set up a special unit headed by Lt. Bert Gerding and began a systematic program of both surveilling and playing dirty tricks on students, faculty, and organizations that they deemed subversive. But in the end, all his special undercover unit really accomplished was to document their own illegality even as they provided posterity with an amazingly rich window into 1960s and 1970s counterculture in Austin, for the Bert Gerding files ended up at the University of Texas and now count as one of the most important sources of primary information we have about that era.[16]

On the questionnaire about subversive organizations at the pre-induction physical, I noted that I had attended the national convention of the SDS recently held in Austin, but only as a registered guest. Red flags and alarm bells! After all the physical examinations were completed, I was singled out and asked if I objected to being fingerprinted, to which, once again somewhat naively, I replied, "No." After that I was given forms to fill out asking all sorts of questions about the nature of my relationship to the SDS, the Communist Party, and other subversive groups in general. I thought that was the end of it, but it was, rather, the beginning. The officer in charge then solemnly announced that it would be necessary for me to stay over and come back in the morning and answer questions by an officer of Military Intelligence and that a voucher for a hotel room would be issued to that end. I was put up that night at the Montagu Hotel where inductees were temporarily billeted by the army.

The following day I was interviewed by one Charles Ray of Military Intelligence, a dull, tired man with pale blue eyes, but not altogether unsympathetic—apparently an important trait for interrogators. He asked me all sorts of questions concerning my beliefs and stance about the war, which I was more than willing to answer, and I got the impression that he was rather startled to have someone in front of him who had well-formed opinions and had the ability to articulate them clearly and precisely. On one occasion he tried to counter me by reciting an army saying, but when he got halfway through he forgot the second half, which was awkward for us both. I also had to fill out an official witness form (DA Form 2823), which included a series of questions offering real insight into the paranoia that existed within the military at the time.

> Question: At the time you attended these meetings were you aware that the SDS was considered by the US government to be an organization that was controlled or strongly influenced by individuals or foreign governments that are hostile toward the American Way of Life?

Answer: No. (See appendix 1.)

I spent the rest of the day waiting around for my answers to be typed up, which I looked over and signed, and after that I was released, but the story was not over. The army, I subsequently became convinced, was keeping a close eye on me, and this particular episode would resurface at a later date in Vietnam.

As I look back now and reflect on my own run-ins with the FBI and Military Intelligence, it becomes so clear to me that student activists of the period and the various organizations that sought to mobilize them, including the SDS, never posed any serious threat to the American way of life. The SDS convention that I had attended provided a case in point: the organization had fractured in front of me and ceased from that point in time to be an effective force, a victim of its own internal squabbling, which is the usual trajectory for organizations of this nature. On the contrary, the real threat always lay within the various intelligence agencies themselves, which, taking their lead from the irrational paranoia of J. Edgar Hoover and his COINTELPRO program, systematically prejudiced and compromised the Constitution they were sworn to uphold. When all is said and done, what was more subversive? What was needed then as now on the part of our leaders was not so much "intelligence" as wisdom. They also needed a crash course in the US Constitution. Unfortunately, this sad condition has only worsened with time.

Perhaps the interview with Military Intelligence was the catalyst, who knows. But soon thereafter the clouds parted and the skies cleared: the war was completely wrong; I could not be a part of it. Signing up with the ROTC as a means of forestalling the inevitable had been a double fraud: for the Army a con job and for myself a betrayal. So I wrote a letter requesting withdrawal from the program, which was granted. I also wrote to my local draft board a week after my examination requesting SSS Form 150, the official application form for CO status.

I was beginning to fit almost exactly the official profile drawn up by the SSS in 1969 for the new breed of CO that both they and the army viewed with alarm:

- Registrant did not claim conscientious objection when he completed his classification questionnaire (after turning eighteen).
- Registrant is a college graduate or attended college several years and withdrew.
- Registrant has been in a deferred status, usually II-S, for several years, and sometime has held another deferment, such as II-A, for a period of time.
- Registrant is ordered for induction.
- Registrant claims c.o. [conscientious objector status], and requests Form 150 (at this point, after he has received an induction order, it seems that the registrant has consulted friends, possibly a draft counselor, or has obtained information from another source in which he has discovered that, if the c.o. claim is filed, his induction can be postponed until his claim has been reviewed).
- Registrant files [SSS] Form 150. He shows some degree of religious training and background derived from his parents and early religious training in church. Sometimes this is continued on into

his college years. He then acknowledges that organized religion is no longer a part of his life and that, after much study, he has come to have some doubts about many facets of organized religion. However, during the last two years, after much discussion with friends and teachers, he has adopted a personal approach toward religious beliefs and he is now committed to the philosophy of "love," "humanism." His life is based on this principle. He says that his beliefs have only crystallized or become mature during the past few years, but he had this feeling, although dormant, all along. Most supporting letters come from friends and acquaintances from the past two years; very rarely are there any supporting letters from persons who have known the registrant eight or ten years. ... Most correspondents testify to the sincerity of the registrant but offer little or no more substantial proof.[17]

I made a special trip home to inform my parents of my decision. It was a stormy meeting: they were upset, to put it mildly, and their complete lack of understanding was extremely painful for me. I loved my parents and deeply appreciated the support and encouragement they had shown and the sacrifices they had made on behalf of both my brother and me over the years. But I was saddened and even embittered that they could find no understanding and sympathy for the ethical dilemma I faced and that they appeared to place community status above parental support. It marked the beginning of a serious breach that took many years to heal.

Shaped by the hardships and sacrifices characteristic of the Great Depression and the World War II years, both had worked hard—my mother as a schoolteacher and my father as a rancher—to improve their lot in life both financially and socially. They had been successful at both. Their growing prosperity had even enabled them to underwrite fully undergraduate educations for my brother and me. The Kearneys could hold their heads high, and we all did so.

But holding one's head high implied sharing the values of the very conservative community where we had made our home for generations and not rocking the boat in any obvious way. My application for CO status was sure to do that. Columbus, my hometown, is located in a big bend of the Colorado River, and had been one of the main centers of plantation slave culture in antebellum Texas. During my youth the town and county seemed to be locked in the past, as if in a museum. Several stately antebellum houses reminded us of this legacy daily, while the United Daughters of the Confederacy counted as one of the most prominent social clubs in town. Segregation was still absolute during my youth; indeed, my high school class, the class of 1964, was the last to be fully segregated nearly ten years after the landmark *Brown v. Board of Education* (1954), which ostensibly ended the practice.

It was also a very patriotic community, as most rural communities are. But Columbus and Colorado County could not avoid the winds of change forever, and the conservative mindset, which seemed to be well-nigh ubiquitous among the white population, recoiled in horror at the inexorable changes visible on the horizon. This mindset viewed the growing agitation for civil rights among Black people and the growing antiwar movement as one and the same, which was not far from the truth. So to them those who burned their draft cards, or refused induction, or applied for CO status were not only cowards and traitors but also civil rights agitators, and it is not clear which they reviled the most.

For me, however, the connection to civil rights had not yet been made. Even at this stage, regretfully, I had still not entirely freed myself from the prejudices that I had grown up with, and my activism was focused entirely on the war. Sadly, I had never really associated with a Black person on fully equal terms until, ironically, I joined the army. It was a new experience for me, and here, for the first time, it began to dawn on me what a horrible and degrading system segregation had been, and I was baffled that I could have been so indifferent to its injustices for so long.

The SSS Form 150, referenced in the official profile above, was the document used to request CO status. It framed the CO experience for thousands upon thousands of young men during the Vietnam era.

You were asked to sign one of two claims for exemption and then document your claim:

> I am, by reason of my religious training and belief, conscientiously opposed to participation in war in any form. I, therefore, claim exemption from combatant training and service in the Armed Forces, but am prepared to serve in a noncombatant capacity if called. (Registrants granted this status are classified I-A-O.)
>
> (Signature of registrant)
>
> I am, by reason of my religious training and belief, conscientiously opposed to participation in war in any form and I am further conscientiously opposed to participation in noncombatant training and service in the Armed Forces. I, therefore, claim exemption from both combatant and noncombatant training and service in the Armed Forces, but am prepared to perform civilian alternative service if called. (Registrants granted this status are classified I-O.)
>
> (Signature of registrant)[18]

I chose to check the first box, which immediately begs the question, why would one choose the first box and apply for 1-A-O rather than 1-O status? For the religious minded, especially Seventh Day Adventists, this was a choice dictated by their religious beliefs, but for me, this represented a compromise that I was willing to make. Deep down I believed in service to one's country, and I understand now that this was a defining characteristic of most 1-A-Os, whether political or religious. I was deeply sensitive to being called a coward, or a shirker, or a CO by reason of "expediency." I could see beyond Vietnam and did not want that label attached to me for the rest of my life. I even saw it as a way to protect the family name and shield my parents from the kind of shame they might feel.

The reader will quickly note that application to either status, 1-O or 1-A-O, was predicated on two essential criteria: the "religious training and belief" requirement and the "conscientiously opposed to participation in war in any form" requirement. These requirements had remained essentially unchanged since the implementation of the Selective Training and Service Act of 1940 and never encountered serious legal challenges until the Vietnam era. Both presented problems for me: first, my objection to the Vietnam War, and my participation in it, was entirely secular/ethical/political rather than "by reason of religious training and belief," and secondly, I was not opposed to all wars, just to this one. On the surface of it, I should have been turned down, but a recent Supreme Court decision, *United States v. Seeger* (1965), which I was not even aware of at the time, came to my rescue, at least partially. This court case, and others, had forced the SSS to loosen the basic requirements for CO status even though the wording remained essentially unaltered. But this loosening was not general knowledge; certainly, I had no inkling of it.

Prior to Vietnam two unwritten but well-understood corollaries also colored all applications for CO status, which most draft boards clearly understood and routinely applied. The first corollary favored members of historically pacifist churches, principally the Amish, Mennonites, Quakers, Herrnhuter, and a plethora of smaller sects. Moreover, you had to be born into these denominations and not have converted at a later date out of "expediency," a dirty word for draft boards. The 1940 law did not outright exclude members of mainline denominations such as (say) Roman Catholics or Methodists, but acceptance was not at all routine since local draft boards often took a dim view of such applications. This prejudice, likewise, began to crumble during the Vietnam War.

The second corollary reserved 1-A-O status (noncombatant within the military) for those peace churches that also permitted service in the military, and of these, the Seventh Day Adventists stand out. Indeed, the crafters of the 1940 Selective Service Act most assuredly had the Seventh Day Adventists in mind when they created this special status. This is because their unusual belief system mandated both service and pacifism, the only religious sect known to me to do so. Seventh Day

Adventists always made up 40 percent or more of 1-A-O medics.[19] *Hacksaw Ridge*, a recent Hollywood film about the extraordinary heroism of Desmond Doss, one of the most decorated soldiers in the Pacific theater in World War II and a 1-A-O medic and Seventh Day Adventist, illustrates this point.

Unaware of the legal ramifications of the Seeger case or that draft boards across the nation had received a confidential memorandum from the SSS informing them that, henceforth, deeply held ethical convictions of a personal nature could substitute for "religious train-ing and belief," I took the wording on the form at face value and recognized this to be a serious problem for me. That I believed this is clearly shown by an answer I gave on the witness form during my interrogation by Military Intelligence:

Q: Do you have any objection to being inducted into the US Armed Forces under the current laws governing the induction of personnel for the US Armed Forces?

A: In principal [*sic*], I profoundly disagree to being inducted into the US Armed Services because I am thoroughly and unequiv-ocally opposed to the present war in Vietnam and under pres-ent law I cannot become a conscientious objector on other than religious grounds. Since the alternative is three years in prison, I will probably accept induction. This government together with the other allied powers of World War II tried and put to death Germans for not following their consciousness [*sic*] instead of their leaders. Yet when Americans do follow their conscience, they are thrown in jail. This seems to me to show some hipocracy [*sic*]. (See appendix 1.)

My solution was to approach the Methodist preacher in Columbus, Greg Robertson, who happened to be a distant relative, and to ask him to write a letter attesting to the sincerity of my beliefs, even though I had never personally set foot in his church since he had assumed the pastorage. Nevertheless, he consented to talk with me, and after several sessions where we discussed my beliefs in detail, he agreed to my request. In the letter he penned, he cleverly drew a contrast between myself and my brother, a recent graduate of Texas A&M, who had just entered the army himself as a second lieutenant under the ROTC program. (The letter is reproduced in appendix 2.)

There was one other strike against me. The law required (and still requires) that all males register with the SSS when they turn eighteen. This I had dutifully done at the local post office, where a standard form to that purpose was available. This form included the question, "Are you conscientiously opposed to war in any form due to religious training and belief?"[20] I checked the "No" box at the time, unaware that I had seriously compromised any subsequent application for CO status. It is, of course, absurd to think that one's ethical or moral consciousness cannot grow or mature beyond his eighteenth birthday, but the way the SSS viewed it, any subsequent application for CO status always smelled of "expediency," ipso facto a cause for rejection.

I had been reclassified 1-A (eligible for service) on March 6, 1969, and ordered to report to the Army Induction Center in Houston on April 3. Between these dates, I filed for 1-A-O status and requested a postponement of my induction pending the outcome of my application. My draft board, Texas Local Board #44, met in the neighboring county in the town of La Grange. I actually expected that my local draft board would turn my request down. I believed the cards to be stacked against me on three counts: on the "religious belief and training" requirement, on the "opposition to all wars" requirement, and because I had checked the "No" box when I turned eighteen. Furthermore, I was making application to a rural Texas draft board where, to my knowledge, no one had ever before made application or had been granted CO status.

I also knew the president of the board, Sam K. Seymour III, very well—too well—since I had worked at his hardware store one summer when in high school and had become very familiar with his iron-clad conservative and unnuanced outlook on the world. In addition to being head of the local draft board, Mr. Sam, as he was known, was commander of the local VFW (Veterans of Foreign Wars), chairman of the Colorado County Democratic Party, president of the local chamber of commerce, and owner of several other businesses around town; in a word, the most prominent citizen of the county. He had also served in the famed Rainbow Division in World War I and was a personal friend of LBJ. His support for the war was unconditional. That he would view my application favorably was unlikely.

But I had a fallback plan. At some point—I can't remember exactly when—I made application for graduate school in the Department of Germanic Studies at the University of British Columbia in Vancouver. I had an acceptance letter in hand with an offer for a teaching assist-antship and was quite prepared to take the leap. I often reflect on how utterly different my life's journey would have been. Would I have come to regret it, perhaps bitterly so? Would I ever have reconciled with my family? Would I ever have been able to come back to the ranch where I had grown up and where I had a deep emotional attachment that only those who are deeply rooted to the land can understand? My whole future hung upon the decision of my local board.

Against all expectations, the board voted in my favor, and as I look back, I think the one consideration that swayed them was simply that I was neither trying to avoid military service nor, once admitted, angling to escape combat duty. The board was perfectly aware that 99 percent of 1-A-Os were trained as army medics and that, ironi-cally, to be granted 1-A-O status greatly increased one's likelihood for combat duty.[21] Most assuredly, this swayed draft boards across the country to begin approving exactly the new brand of political COs that the Army subsequently found troubling. I remain convinced, at least, this was the case for me.

It was with a big sigh of relief that I received the news. I felt like a bargain had been struck. Yes, it was a compromise, but it was one that I could live with, and I resolved to uphold my part of the deal and hoped the army would do the same. I would be good soldier Kearney. The board only met once a month in the middle of the month. By the time my application was complete, put on the agenda, and approved, it was already June. They then ordered me to report to the Army Induc-tion Center in Houston the following month, on July 8, 1969.

Chapter 2

You're in the Army Now
Training at Fort Sam Houston
(*Kearney*)

For the induction I packed a light bag and hopped a bus for Houston. The Greyhound bus terminal, as I recall, was only a block or so from the induction center. After checking in, completing a round of paper work, and waiting around for it to be processed, I was grouped with all the others scheduled for that day. We were lined up and asked to step forward, raise our hands, and swear an oath of allegiance to the United States and to the US Military:

> I, (NAME), do solemnly swear (or affirm) that I will support and defend the Constitution of the United States against all enemies, foreign and domestic; that I will bear true faith and allegiance to the same; and that I will obey the orders of the President of the United States and the orders of the officers appointed over me, according to regulations and the Uniform Code of Military Justice. So help me God.[1]

The officer in charge then congratulated us with the little speech, "You're now in the US Military. You're subject to legal orders and entitled to military pay and benefits." In other words, as the song goes:

> You're in the Army now.
> You're not behind a plow.
> And remember, from now on,
> if you're early, you're on time.
> If you're on time, you're late,
> and if you're late, you're dead.

After the ceremony we waited around for orders and travel vouchers to whatever base across the country we had been assigned for basic training. Finally, my name was called, and I was astonished and alarmed to see that I had orders for Fort Bliss in El Paso rather than Fort Sam Houston in San Antonio. Knowing that all 1-A-O medics took basic training at Fort Sam Houston, why had I received orders for Fort Bliss? Did the army really intend to live up to its side of the bargain? I had been in the army only a few hours and was already confronting a situation that didn't bode well for the future. However, my fears were misplaced, and what appeared at first blush to be a breach of trust was in reality an early initiation into army inefficiency: the right hand, as I discovered over and over again, very often did not know what the left hand was doing. This was clearly the case here, as it turned out, resulting in a convoluted trip from Houston to San Antonio by way of El Paso.

The flight to El Paso was memorable because I was seated next to a young Black inductee from rural East Texas who had never flown on an airplane before and who was quite visibly petrified with fear in the moments leading to takeoff. I did my best to reassure him and calm him down, but not until we were safely airborne and had leveled off at cruising altitude did he release his ironclad grip on his seat and unclench the muscles in his face. After that we settled in for an uneventful flight and enjoyed a pleasant conversation.

Once we had arrived in El Paso and been transported to the base, the sergeant in charge ushered us into a transit barracks for incoming recruits. The next day they issued us uniforms and a duffle bag to carry all our earthly possessions. Then we sat down for a series of tests in order to determine our aptitudes, skills, and preferences. We also filled out questionnaires about our employment and educational backgrounds. I think I was the only one among the inductees who had a college degree, and at twenty-three I certainly counted as one of the older among the recruits. The purpose of all this was to help the army assign us a military occupational specialty (MOS) that more or less lined up with the aptitude, skills, and education of the recruit. The tests, a whole battery of them, began immediately, and I took them along with everyone else. But there was one problem: by becoming a 1-A-O, my MOS was already predetermined to be 91A10, combat medic, so there was really no sense in taking these exams. I mentioned this to the officer in charge and a perplexed look came over his face. He acknowledged that I did not belong and would bring it to the attention of his superiors. Sure enough, the next day I received a bus ticket to San Antonio where I should have been sent in the first place.

At the time the army existed on carbon copies and mimeograph machines and required a clerical army-within-the-army to keep up with all the files and reams of paper work generated. Typically, when a soldier transferred from one duty station to another, he hand carried a packet containing all his paper work, which was then dutifully handed over to the clerk of the executive officer at the new duty station. The one-year tour of duty, one of the oddities that set Vietnam apart, compounded the paper work nightmare; no longer in for the duration, over a million soldiers passed through the revolving door of Vietnam service, and the amount of paper work that this generated would surely fill a canyon. Seen in this light, my little snafu was not unusual, but still I often wondered how a new duty station knew that I was 1-A-O; I never found any special code or indication in my paper work identifying me as such. Each time I got a new assignment, I simply told someone in charge, usually a senior noncommissioned officer (NCO), and that was all it took.

After three days in limbo in El Paso, I hopped a Greyhound bus back to San Antonio. It was a pleasant trip. It had been a wet spring, and once as we passed over the Llano River bridge at the town of Junction, putting the barrenness of the Trans-Pecos and the monotony of the Edwards Plateau in the rearview mirror, we entered the distinctive Texas Hill Country, and the charm of the new landscape could not fail to impress: steep hills, sharp ravines, clear flowing streams, magnificent cypress trees and live oaks bedecked with Spanish moss, and fields of wildflowers of all shades and colors.

Fort Sam Houston in San Antonio is one of the more charming military bases in the country. Constructed after the Civil War, it now occupies nearly three thousand acres just to the north and east of downtown San Antonio. The base is practically in the center of the larger metroplex that has grown up around it. It preserves one of the largest collections of historic nineteenth-century military buildings of any military base in the United States and many are still in use. Ample green spaces separate the rows of two-story Victorian-era buildings used to house officers and senior NCOs, while the main parade ground, the very one where my father's horse bolted during final review so many years before, is over a mile long and several hundred yards wide.

One of the ironies about Fort Sam Houston is that it is actually named for a CO of sorts, something clearly understood in 1876 when the base was established and named after Sam Houston, the name being salt in the wound for die-hard ex-Confederates in Texas. What, you say, Sam Houston, the hero of San Jacinto, the Father of Texas, a CO? Old Sam was, in fact, an uncompromising Unionist who had resigned as governor rather than take the oath of allegiance to the Confederacy. Moreover, he had prophesied correctly in his farewell speech that the war would end in calamitous defeat, an unmitigated disaster for the South and Texas. He died a short time thereafter reviled by the very citizens who once celebrated him. This story was fresh on the minds of Texans in 1876 when the fort was established.

The role of Fort Sam Houston has changed with the times. Originally for infantry and cavalry units, it witnessed the birthplace of military aviation prior to World War I. At the end of World War II, the army brass decided to repurpose the fort and make it the principal medical training facility, with Brooke Army Medical Center as its centerpiece. Thereafter, the fort came to be known as the Home of Army Medicine and Home of the Combat Medic. This was certainly the case during the Vietnam War. The army set aside a special, self-contained compound in the heart of the old part of the fort to train combat medics. It was a major operation, and every year thousands of freshly minted medics graduated from the facility headed mainly for the revolving door of Vietnam.

Within this complex existed another smaller compound with its own barracks, classrooms, dining hall, and command structure. The purpose of this compound, designated Echo 4, was to provide basic training to the incoming 1-A-Os, which lasted a total of six weeks. This training was essentially the same as for all other army inductees with the exception that there was no weapons training. Echo 4 had ten separate classes that averaged about thirty-five trainees per class. They were staggered in a such a way that each week a new class began and an old class graduated, and at any given time there were about 350 to 400 trainees in the program. Once the basic training was completed, the 1-A-Os integrated into the larger medical training program and were no longer segregated. Over the course of the Vietnam years, and while the draft was in effect, about ten thousand 1-A-Os graduated from the program, as near as can be estimated, and as a rough figure comprised about 10 percent of all medics at any given time in the army, but it should be noted that the proportion of 1-A-Os gradually increased during the war.[2]

Basic training introduces you to the army and its ways. It is where you learn to salute, march, shine your shoes, polish your brass, and show proper deference to everyone who outranks you, which as a private first class (or E-1) meant basically everybody on the fort outside your own classmates. Basic training is also the place where

Echo 4, basic training at Fort Sam Houston.

you shape up physically and mentally, which means lots of push-ups, forced marches, long days and sleep-deprived nights, and much shouting and dressing down by drill instructors (DIs) for minor infractions. This was all completely novel for most of my classmates, and the adjustment was often not easy.

The first thing the DIs did for a new class was to appoint two class leaders. For our class they picked Fred Ervin to be platoon sergeant—an excellent choice. A Black man from rural Texas, the son of a Baptist preacher, and the tallest in our class, he was also a man of genuine sincerity and obvious integrity and had a certain presence that commanded respect. I was chosen to be assistant platoon sergeant. I never advertised my prior experience with the corps of cadets at Texas A&M to the two DIs in charge of our company, but they had probably noticed from the get-go that I was rather at ease with military expectations and for this reason singled me out for a leadership role, although Bill Clamurro insists it was because I was the second tallest in the class.

Fred and I bunked together in a special space in our barracks. We had the responsibility thrust on us for rousing the recruits at first call in the morning (4:30 a.m.), getting them into formation by 5:00 a.m., marching them to breakfast at 6:00 a.m., marching them from venue to venue during the course of the day, and finally, after arranging a roster for nighttime fire duty—at least two people had to be awake at all times during the night—getting everyone settled in for lights out at 9:00 p.m. sharp. While marching, we had to call cadence, and one of the lyrics we used for double time was:

> Howdy, howdy, hidey ho,
> Howdy, howdy, hidey ho,
> First they teach you how to kill,
> Then they teach you how to heal

Fred was torn between the duty to serve his country and his sincere pacifism. The 1-A-O classification, he felt, had allowed him to reconcile these two convictions. This internal conflict, I came to realize, was a common thread for many 1-A-O medics. Andrew Phelan, another classmate, put it succinctly in the book he subsequently published about his Vietnam experiences: "When I entered the Army, I was reluctantly convinced that I was doing my civic and patriotic duty even as I felt coerced. I was not a supporter of the Vietnam war, but I was an American, and in those days, I believed in the concept of service."[3]

On the whole the DIs were more humane than their counterparts at Texas A&M, but they did not baby us by any means. They did their fair share of shouting and dressing down for minor infractions, or calling out a recruit to drop down and give him a hundred (push-ups, that is) and so forth and so on, but they often did it with a wink and a smile, which never happened at A&M. Indeed, in respect to mental hazing, the US Army did not compare to what I had experienced at Texas A&M, and so, already well-conditioned to hazing, I fared better than most. For several of the fresh inductees, however, adjustment to military life came as a rude shock, both mentally and physically, and drove some to the breaking point. One recruit stands out in my memory who, in the middle of a classroom, suddenly sprang from his chair and bolted for the screen door, which was shut. He didn't bother to open it, knocking it off its hinges. Once outside he continued his flight. We never saw him again, and whatever the army decided to do with him, we never heard.

My friendship with Bill Clamurro, the coauthor of this book, began in basic training. Bill Clamurro hailed from a sophisticated Italian-American family from Nutley, New Jersey, right across the river from the Big Apple. Something of a prodigy in high school, he had gained entrance into prestigious Amherst College, where he majored in literature. Bill had taken up the oboe in high school and was proficient enough to join the college orchestra while at Amherst. Music always being an important part of his life, he has maintained his orchestra-grade proficiency through daily practice to the present day, participating in numerous university orchestras and chamber groups over the years. By the time he was drafted, he had also completed his master's degree in English literature at the University of Washington.

Bill and I had discovered over the course of the sixteen weeks or so that we were together at Fort Sam Houston that despite our radically different backgrounds, we enjoyed each other's company. We became more conscious of this affinity as time passed, so that by the end of basic/AIT it was safe to say we had become fast friends. Bill was (and is) a very articulate guy. I wrote in my journal at the time about being spellbound by the ease with which he could verbally dissect the most complicated issues. The right words were always there, the phrasing always brilliant, the effect often intoxicating. Such a talent! I was jealous but recognized a danger—namely, the tendency to simply acquiesce to any point of view Bill took, whether I agreed or not, simply because he articulated it so eloquently.

Bill also had another characteristic that has endeared him to others throughout his life but became his calling card in the army:

an extraordinary sense of humor. The absurdities, indignities, and everyday aggravations of basic training that greeted us at every turn became the stuff of humor rather than the cause of incessant griping so typical of most trainees. The humor cheered our little group on more than one occasion to see our way through our ordeals. Bill also resembled strongly the famous comedian Groucho Marx: a long, curved nose, a bushy, dark moustache—the Army allowed mous-taches then—bright, intelligent eyes, and an infectious laugh. Bill cultivated this likeness, and just like the real Groucho, his humor often took the form of very sophisticated word plays, of turning phrases inside out to reveal their absurdity. He soon earned the nick-name Groucho, and Groucho's reputation, as we shall see, spread far and wide.

But there were, and still are, two Bills. Underneath the humor was a serious and brooding side, which comes through in his Vietnam poems. They often strike me as deep meditations on the major themes of life: loves and friendships made and lost, connections to place culti-vated and severed, time and decay, but all expressed in the context of a senseless war. Selected poems from his Vietnam collection form an essential complement to my own narrative.

In the course of basic training, four members from our class emerged as the nucleus of the political as opposed to religious 1-A-Os. But here an important word of explanation is in order because the distinction is more complicated and nuanced than the two descriptors would suggest. What is really meant is that one's belief system was arrived at freely and independently as a result of a personal journey of ethical discovery and not as the result of "religious training and belief." In this sense *political* did not preclude a religious compo-nent, although this was very often secondary. Bill's belief system, for instance, definitely included a Christian component.

In addition to Bill Clamurro and myself, only Andrew Phelan and another man, who asked to remain anonymous, counted as political 1-A-Os. There may have been a couple more, but we were always a distinct minority. Interestingly, the four of us had all graduated with degrees in the liberal arts, whereas many of our more religious-oriented classmates had only recently graduated from high school. Thus, in addition to being more politically engaged, we were older and more educated than most of our fellow trainees. The four of us took to hanging out together. We were only allowed on-base passes on Sundays during basic, and we would often while away the time at a base pizzeria while most of our comrades attended religious services.

We epitomized the new type of CO that Capt. James R. Castleberry, the commander of Echo 4, characterized as a new and troubling breed of 1-A-Os who were "lowering the caliber" of COs in the army. He made these comments in an article about Echo 4, which was syndicated in major newspapers across the country while we were taking our training.[4] The article was entitled "Echo 4 Co. at Ft. Sam Houston Is Most Unorthodox Unit in U.S. Army." The political nature of our opposition to the war, taken together with significant age and educational differences, became a defining factor for both Bill and me in our army experience. It set us apart from even our fellow 1-A-Os with whom, on the surface, we appeared to have so much in common.

The Texas heat was a challenge, especially for those from the more northern climes, who appeared to form the majority of the trainees. Neither the barracks nor the classrooms had air conditioning, and it often became a real challenge to stay awake in the hot, stuffy, and unventilated classrooms, especially since we all felt perpetually sleep-deprived. Bill Clamurro made the heat during basic training the focus of the first of many poems he wrote during his army experience. Bill was actually born in San Antonio. His father served in the US Army Air Corps and had been temporarily stationed there with his young wife during the waning days of World War II.

San Antonio, Summer 1969

July in San Antonio, unforgiving
Texas heat. By a grim coincidence

I've returned to where I was born.
An eerie similarity: it was the ending

of another very different war.
April 1945, a war that had
a clarity of ends, a finality
that all the later ones would lack.

And here, we were a paradox, training
to be soldiers without weapons,
destined to be medics, an unarmed
contradiction in a conflict, a catastrophe.

The jungle heat would come later, but this
was a crucible. At the end of each day
we'd wash in the big group shower room,
our tired bodies briefly soothed, redeemed,

a coolness we'd come to value even more
as Vietnam opened but didn't complete its story,
while here, stripped of more than uniforms,
we'd be prepared through forced obedience.

For my part, as I noted in my journal at the time, the heat, the physical exertion, and the lack of sleep all served to keep me distracted from "love's labor lost"—still a foolish and wasteful preoccupation for me—and so, in an odd way, all the discomfort of basic training served as a welcome diversion. Indeed, physical exhaustion is usually the best cure for a troubled mind and a broken heart. I also noted in my journal on July 20 that Apollo 11 had landed safely and, for the first time, men had walked on the moon. Considering what a momentous event this was, I was surprised at how little attention it received among the trainees. We were too absorbed by our own situation, I suppose, to have much time for discussion and reflection.

Our class graduated from basic training on September 5 and immediately began AIT as medics. At this time we mixed in with the rest of the trainees, but the majority of our class stayed together in Company D, 3rd Battalion. On September 17, I and other former classmates from Class 3, Echo 4, were promoted to private second class (E-2). The promotion list, which I have kept, is the only partial roster I could find for Class 3, Echo 4, and so is a valuable record of the period.

It became possible to obtain off-base and even weekend passes during AIT, and I took advantage of this to organize a couple of week-end trips for my newfound buddies. This was possible because I had a car, which had I parked (illegally) at an out-of-the-way spot on the base. One weekend I invited our group—Bill Clamurro, Andrew Phelan, and one other colleague—to come to the family ranch, which was only a two-hour drive east of San Antonio. We stayed at a camp house on one of the two ranches my father owned, which stood empty most of the year and was several miles distant from the family home and headquarters. We spent most of the time sitting on the porch

88 Ranch camp house.

talking about all sorts of things while watching deer and cattle grazing
in the distance.

Camphouse, October 13, 1969

Wind slants over the tireless fields,
The grass alive with animals,
The dust and clasping seeds;

The building settles beyond a recall
To the whistling of trees
And the continuing laws
Of burnished crickets and the waddling
Armadillos; the long dusk falls
And singular warm night
Grows deeper on the mind,

As the wind moves
Undiminished, threading cabins
With the wind blades
Of a mill. And night.

The bringing together of
These others and their isolated thoughts.
The shifting result of stars
Is far too grand on prairies
Where men leave mystery of the night
To the night itself.

Or now the wind stirs
Through the sure and fading gray
Of the cow skull hanging on a tree;
The splintering of silver planking
On this southward scanning porch
Tells partly of an aging
In a cabin's silent, antlered space.

The skies grow terrible,
A livid orange, momentarily

And as shapeless as our fear,
Our waiting for the violence,

An impossible time that divides us,
Like the thin, iron knife
Into the futility of the labyrinth.

But curtains gesture over the sills,
The signals of the motive wind
Indifferent to eyes in southward
Searching, men in the fragments
Of their thoughts.

The resonance of wars and inner wars
That drift upon the pulse
Of the tireless prairie into night.

I have often been asked how the army went about preparing us to become combat medics with life-and-death responsibilities. A typical day included classroom instruction, usually in the form of a film, then a demonstration, and finally hands-on practice, where we partnered up and practiced on one another. We were not issued a textbook, as I recall, which is odd, since the army actually had a manual tailored specifically for combat medics that covered all the procedures we were supposed to master. I only became aware of this manual once I was in-country, when I inherited a copy from the medic I replaced at my first duty station in Vietnam. I found it very useful as a handy reference and remain perplexed about why it was not made more widely available. Our instruction, therefore, included very little extra study, and in this it departed markedly from any schooling at any level I had experienced before. Since nobody could fail, there apparently was little sense in giving and taking exams. Everybody was expected to master the lesson of the day, but the degree to which this actually happened had to be uneven, to say the least.

The program only lasted ten weeks—not a lot of time to absorb the basics of emergency care. Also, since a small percentage of the

Medical training at Fort Sam Houston, 1968. Courtesy Carlos Alvarado, chief archivist, US Army Medical Museum, Fort Sam Houston, San Antonio, Texas.

trainees ended up as hospital orderlies, a portion of the training time (a couple of weeks) focused on teaching the basic duties of being an orderly, such as how to place a bedpan or how to change the sheets with the patient remaining in the bed, and things of this nature. A couple of classes addressed basic sanitation procedures (how to clean things in the field, how to set up latrines, how to treat water to make it potable, etc.), and for me these turned out to be valuable lessons.

The lion's share of our training, however, focused on the skills necessary for a field medic to assess and stabilize traumatic injuries in a battlefield situation. The instructors emphasized the four live-saving techniques: stop the bleeding, clear the airway, protect the wound, and treat for shock. Each of these situations had a toolbox of procedures that had to be mastered. In respect to bleeding, for example, we learned the various ways to apply pressure bandages in combination with gauze and tape, and the correct ways to wrap wounds on different parts of the torso. We also learned the difference between arterial and venal bleeding, which required understanding where the major arteries are located. We learned when and how to use tourniquets and pressure points to quickly stem arterial bleeding, which, if not done in a timely way, can quickly lead to death. In respect to the airway, we learned to insert various tubes, or, in extreme situations, how to do a cricothyroidotomy as an emergency intervention to establish an airway.

Our instructors stressed how critical it was to thoroughly check the patient, especially in the case of those who had shrapnel wounds from grenades or mines. The little splinters of steel often enter the body at extreme velocity, and although they might leave a deceptively small entrance wound, they often do tremendous damage to soft tissue and penetrate deeply into the body. Certain types of wounds, such as sucking chest wounds, called for a tailored response on the part of the medic. In such a wound, the chest cavity loses its vacuum that enables breathing, and so the treatment is not just to stem the bleeding but also to seal the hole (or holes) to prevent death by asphyxiation.

I found the lessons on shock to be particularly interesting, and these lessons led to a growing appreciation of how tough the human body can be and how various defenses and mechanisms have evolved over the millennia to deal with trauma. The word *shock* is misleading for many because it calls to mind so-called shell shock, a psychological state of extreme distress and dysfunction brought on by intense combat situations that often has physical manifestations such as uncontrolled shaking. This is a condition that since the Vietnam War goes by the acronym PTSD (post-traumatic stress disorder). Traumatic shock, in contrast, is a purely physiological response, or reflex, on the part of the human body to extreme loss of blood. Basically, the body shuts down blood flow to extremities to preserve what blood is left for essential organs. Arms and legs become cold and clammy to the touch, making it very difficult to find a pulse or to start an intravenous (IV) solution. In addition to learning how to start IVs, we learned how to do cutdowns in order to deal with just the scenario outlined above. In a cutdown one literally takes a scalpel to open up

My medic's bag.

the skin on (say) the back of the hand to search for a suitable vein to insert an IV. This is, of course, a procedure that only a medical doctor would perform back in "the world," but once we were in the field in Vietnam, we routinely mastered procedures and assumed responsibilities nominally reserved to doctors.

We were not issued the standard US Army M5 medic's bag, as I recall, until we arrived in Vietnam, but once there we quickly realized that it was designed to facilitate the four life-saving steps discussed above. Hence, it contained a large supply and variety of pressure bandages, gauzes, and tape, along with several tubes to help with clogged airways or to insert in the chest cavity. The bag also included splints (sometimes pneumatic) with which to set broken bones, but this was a task usually deferred to rear aid stations since broken bones, though painful, are not as a rule life-threatening. We also had a small surgical kit that included sutures, scalpel, and thread; yes, we found ourselves often doing stitches for minor cuts and wounds. But the blunt-nosed bandage scissors all medics carried were the one item to achieve iconic status. Always prominently displayed in the blouse pockets with the handle sticking out, the little scissors became the universal calling card of all medics throughout Vietnam. Finally, I should mention, we also carried an assortment of drugs, which I will discuss at greater length later. In AIT we received, with the exception of morphine, very little instruction or guidance in the various drugs we carried. In the case of morphine, the instructors simply drilled into us that if there were any hint of trauma to the brain or central nervous system, the drug could not be administered, no matter how severe the pain.

Chapter 3

"I Don't Give a Damn, Next Stop Is Vietnam"
(*Kearney*)

A s AIT drew to an end and we began to ponder what would come next, the last thing our little group did together was to attend a concert in downtown San Antonio, and the performer was none other than Janice Joplin, the local Texas girl who became one of the iconic voices of protest during the Vietnam era. She had created a sensation that very August at Woodstock, the most significant musical festival of a whole generation. A more fitting and poignant end to our Fort Sam Houston experience could not have been imagined.

AIT ended with a formal graduation ceremony where we were all drawn up, company by company, to hear words of praise and encouragement. It reminded me of a Texas pep rally preceding a football game, but this time the losers would be losers for life. The week thereafter notices concerning future assignments began dribbling in piecemeal. Many of the NCOs received duty stateside or in Europe, but one by one all of my former classmates from basic training received orders for Vietnam. There was, of course, a hard logic behind this: presumably, the army didn't care to have odd birds like us either stateside or in Europe where we might stir up dissent, so the easiest solution was to ship us all to Vietnam. After a short orientation about RVN (Republic of Vietnam) service, my former classmates boarded respective planes or buses for a two-week leave before reporting to the big military facility at Oakland, California, from where all army personnel departed for Vietnam.

Letter from Bill Clamurro:
Palo Alto, CA
26 November 1969

Dear Jim,

As you can see, I am in the S.F. area where I will be visiting various old friends until I go, on the 3rd, to Oakland (and then to S. Vietnam). But yesterday when I was in New Jersey, I saw Paul Anderson who told me that (when he left) you were still in R&H, but were also doing the RVN orientation. Do you know at this point where you are to be sent?

Things were all too hurried and confused on that last day; and I very much regret that all our mutual "leave-takings" had to be so perfunctory—in fact, nonexistent. Somehow, again, I had hoped we could have managed it all in a more relaxed and orderly way; or perhaps it is better to hope that at some future time we will have the time to redress such a situation ...

Meanwhile, now I can feel that I'm "not getting out of anything"; and I know that this occasionally gives me a sense of self-pity—or else some self-indulging "moral superiority." But how will we fare? I suspect I'll be followed into some absurd corner of RVN by one of the old-familiar CO faces (quien sabe?), and this may help. If I could choose, I'd rather have you around to help puzzle out the initial strangeness. Why? What difference does/would it make? Don't know: but I suspect it does make a difference ...

Peace and I hope to see you again soon.

Yours,
Bill

It was an abrupt and disquieting situation, which Bill references in his letter: all our newfound friends and comrades vanished, as if it had all been a dream. In the chaotic and hectic rush, we found little time to properly say good-bye and figure out how to stay in contact. People disappeared never to be seen or heard from again. I never saw or spoke to Andrew until fifty years later. Only later did I learn that three of our classmates from basic training had been killed and several wounded. Only with difficulty did Bill and I reestablish communication once in Vietnam. For another colleague, who wishes to remain anonymous, Fort Sam Houston had been ceaselessly miserable. He found the heat and humidity to be oppressive and he suffered terribly from allergies the whole time he was there. Once, when he sought treatment at the base hospital, Brooke Army, which is also where the army's seriously burned are treated, he saw firsthand many of the burn victims from Vietnam, many hideously disfigured, which shocked him deeply. The doctor who examined him, a full colonel, dismissed his complaint with the remark that Texas ragweed, the cause of the allergy, did not grow in Vietnam where he was sure to end up. This experience must have been the final straw for him. Only later did we discover that he used his leave time to desert to Sweden—one of the approximately three hundred soldiers to do so during the war—rather than report for Vietnam duty in Oakland, California.

There was one exception to this disengagement and dispersal from Fort Sam Houston. I alone among all my classmates received no orders at all. I remained behind, day after day without orders, completely mystified. No one seemed to know why, and so they placed me in a temporary barracks (R&H) where I languished, consuming my prom-ised leave time in idleness and limbo for two whole weeks before anything happened. A student of German and history in my academic life, I should have wished for assignment in Germany as my first choice, but that was not the case. It is hard to explain these things, but my newfound friends were all headed for Vietnam and I felt I belonged with them.

It was with an odd sense of relief, then, that after the two-week hiatus, I finally received orders for Vietnam and all the paper work and travel vouchers necessary to get me to Oakland. I often reflect upon this little interlude. Did it in any way connect with my earlier (and future) encounters with Military Intelligence? Because of the delay, I alone among my classmates received no leave time and flew directly from San Antonio to Oakland, where one traded his stateside army uniform for jungle fatigues, jungle boots, a poncho, and a boonie hat.

About Oakland I remember the lines, the waiting, a big room with a TV where a crowd gathered to watch the second manned mission to the moon by Apollo 12 on November 19, 1969, and I often reflect on the poignancy of this coincidence. Vietnam represented the worst of our nation and the moon landings the best, and my life was intersecting with the worst even as the nation and the world celebrated the best. The long flight over a week or so later was broken by a quick stop in Alaska for refueling; thereafter, it was nonstop to Vietnam, to Tan Son Nhut, the huge American air base outside of Saigon. Our classmate Andrew Phelan described the surreal experience of a typical flight ferrying draftees to Vietnam:

> We flew to Vietnam on commercially chartered flights complete with "coffee, tea, or me" stewardesses, who were cute, dressed in trim uniforms complete with short skirts. (As I recall they were well-trained to deflect the often crude and very direct advances of a planeload of GIs going off to war.) The irony of it was not lost on me ... I wrote cryptically in my notebook: "A very strange way to go to war with pretty stewardesses and all the comforts of a civilian flight."[1]

Vietnam is located in the equatorial band between the Tropic of Cancer and the equator, and similar to most such countries, experiences only two real seasons: a dry season and a wet monsoon season. I arrived at the start of the dry season, which runs from October through March, so the oppressive heat and humidity that so many Americans noted as their first impression of the country was not so pronounced, and in any case, being a native Texan, I was acclimatized to heat, and being from South Texas, to oppressive humidity as well.

Once landed at Tan Son Nhut Air Base, we were put on green army buses outfitted with wire screens over the windows to thwart grenade attacks. The busses sped along streets teeming with the irrepressible street life of Saigon—mopeds, bicyclists, ox carts, pedestrians, roadside stalls—headed for the large army base at Long Binh about twenty kilometers east of Saigon. For most it was the first taste of this (to us) exotic and unfathomable land. I remember the chaotic energy of the street life, the ubiquity of the ao dai, a cotton tunic blouse over black trousers worn by the women, the traditional thatched, palm-leaf conical hats known as the *non la* that both men and women wore, and the redness of the soil.

Long Binh, an expansive logistics facility that also served as the headquarters of the US Army Military Assistance Command, Vietnam (known by its acronym, MACV), was the largest US Army base in Vietnam. At its peak in 1969 it held sixty thousand personnel.[2] It was an American island completely enclosed within a perimeter of ugly, menacing barbed wire and sandbagged fortifications, surrounded by a countryside dotted with green rice fields, villages, and family farmsteads nominally under the control of the army and its Vietnamese allies, the Army of the RVN (ARVN), by day, but dominated by the VC by night. The VC had attacked the base twice, first by sappers in 1967, who, to the shock and embarrassment of the army, successfully penetrated the perimeter and destroyed an enormous ammo dump and several helicopters. They attacked again during the Tet offensive in 1968.[3]

The sheer size of the army base at Long Binh drove home the staggering scale of the war and the logistics required to support it. Much of the matériel (tanks, trucks, cannons, etc.) ended up here temporarily after being offloaded from ships in the nearby harbor and before being distributed to the various units in the field. The base also contained a huge scrap pile of shot-up and wrecked vehicles and aircraft deposited in a line that must have stretched for a mile or more—the waste of war made visible and palpable. And it was all the more shocking for me because, as a country boy whose family had scraped and sacrificed for every tractor, every truck, every piece of machinery the ranch possessed, to see so much valuable equipment discarded in such a rude way was mind-blowing.

Mountain of junked vehicles, tanks, and helicopters at
Long Binh Army Base near Saigon.

Upon arrival at the temporary barracks reserved for incoming and departing troops, we were lined up and given our assignments, our whole fate hanging from this arbitrary lineup. The sergeant in charge had been provided a list of requested replacements, which he had on a clipboard; some were for infantry units (bad assignment), some for artillery units or armored units (not good, but not as bad as the former), and some for rear area dispensaries or aid stations (good). When it came my turn on the list, I was assigned to the A Battery, 2/33rd Artillery, 1st Infantry Division, which was not the best assignment but also not the worst by a long shot. It meant I would be outside the wire (i.e., the perimeter defensive ring of a base), at a small FSB (fire support base), but at least I would not be "humping the boonies," living in the mud and filth with the frontline grunts (field infantry) and exposed to the constant danger of ambush and booby traps, the cause of most casualties in Vietnam at the time. After receiving all the requisite paper work, I hopped a deuce-and-a-half, the standard army two-and-a-half-ton truck, for Lai Khe, where the division headquarters of the 1st Infantry was located.

The Department of Defense had sliced South Vietnam into four main operational areas, starting from the demilitarized zone at the top, numbered I through IV. The marines shared responsibility for I Corps with the army's 101st and Americal divisions, while the army and air force took full responsibility for the other three corps. The 1st Infantry Division stationed at Lai Khe was one of two army divisions assigned to III Corps, which was basically that slice of the country encapsulating Saigon and reaching from the coast to the Cambodian border. Lai Khe was about forty miles due north of Saigon in an area of the country where the French had planted numerous large rubber tree plantations during the colonial period, the most famous of which was the large Michelin plantation. They had carved these out of the surrounding triple canopy jungle, which stretched on a level plain from almost the outskirts of Saigon to Cambodia. The 1st Infantry had located its headquarters near Lai Khe in one of the old plantations along Highway 13, known affectionately by most GIs as Thunder Road. The French colonial road ran from Saigon due north toward An Loc, a major town and site of another American support base, and thence on into Cambodia, which, of course, had once been part of larger French Indochina. The Iron Triangle, a 120-square-mile area between Lai Khe and Saigon, had remained an unsubdued stronghold of the Viet Minh during the First Indochina War and persisted as a VC stronghold during the Vietnam War. The corridor along Thunder Road was the scene of many firefights large and small over the years since it also served as one of the main infiltration routes from sanctuaries in Cambodia and Laos into the Saigon area. The road also offered the VC and NVA ample opportunities for ambushing the daily supply convoys traversing the corridor between Lai Khe and Tay Ninh. Three artillery FSBs, known as Thunder(s) I, II, and III, had been strategically positioned along the road between Lai Khe and An Loc at ten-to-fifteen-mile intervals to provide interlocking support for the ground units out on patrol and to reinforce one another, should one or the other come under attack.

As luck would have it, my classmates and I arrived in country just after the Tet Offensive had fizzled out. The VC and NVA from a strictly military perspective had miscalculated badly and, as a result, had suffered horrendous losses. Although the area of my first assignment had been one of the main concentrations of VC activity in South Vietnam and the site of many pitched battles, the area had settled into a period of relative quiet while both the VC and NVA retrenched and licked their wounds. The army brass, seemingly unable to comprehend the war except in terms of dry statistics, such as body counts and captured weapons, had foolishly misinterpreted this as a defeat so complete that "Charlie" would never be able to recover. ("Charlie" was a ubiquitous slang term used for the enemy, whether VC or NVA, or a combination thereof.) How wrong they were in this assessment only became clear later on, but for the first months of my stay in Vietnam, at least, the countryside had settled into an unnatural lull between storms. But by this I do not mean that people had stopped dying. During the Tet Offensive both the VC and the NVA had launched battalion-sized ground attacks on several American bases in the area, including An Loc, Tay Ninh, and FSB Crook, all within III Corps. Our own battery had even repulsed a smaller ground attack only a week or so before I came into country. Large-scale attacks, however, had ceased completely during my tenure, but the war very much survived as a smoldering ambush war. The VC and the NVA continued to infiltrate by night from their refuges in Cambodia and Laos, lying in wait with ambushes and booby traps by day, using the dense jungle that stretched from Cambodia all the way to the outskirts of Saigon as cover, while the US Army, employing platoon-size infantry and armored patrols, engaged in a constant cat-and-mouse game that continued to produce substantial casualties on both sides.

I checked in at the aid station at Lai Khe, which played a support role for all the medics in the 1st Infantry Division. Here I was issued the standard medic's bag and all the drugs and bandages that went with it, including morphine. I was surprised to discover that there was no doctor present at the aid station; it was staffed entirely by medics, the ranking man being an E-6, or staff sergeant. From that

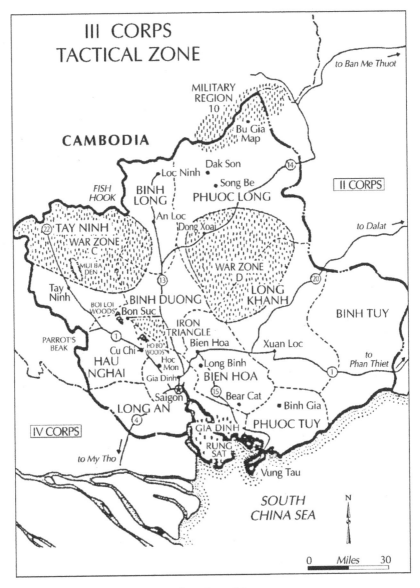

Map of III Corps Vietnam.

point to the end of my tour in Vietnam, I never had any meaningful supervision from a real MD while outside the wire. I learned by doing and watching. The medics took care of just about everything short of intensive care, at which point the real doctors took over. We even dispensed drugs that only real MDs would be permitted to prescribe stateside. In addition to morphine, I carried the antidiarrheal Lomotil, the antipsychotic Thorazine, the anaphylactic epinephrine, and the amphetamine Dexedrine.

The use (and misuse) of prescription drugs by the army in Vietnam is a story in itself, but I was always stuck by the profound irony inherent in the drug situation in Vietnam that seemed to exactly mirror the criminal stupidity of the so-called war on drugs stateside.[4] One reads over and over about the misuse of illegal drugs in Vietnam by the draftees—which, of course, was undeniable—but legal drugs were also abused, especially the mind-altering amphetamines, the narcotic pain killers, and the powerful antipsychotic drugs routinely dispensed to the troops in the field. These had the effect of momentarily suppressing the stress of combat, only to have these stresses reemerge as an epidemic of PTSD among Vietnam veterans for years thereafter. This sad outcome underscores a central fact about war that our politicians never seem to grasp: war does not end once peace is declared, at least for those who participate, and the true costs of a war to society continue to pay negative dividends for decades long after the ink has dried on the peace treaties and the soldiers have returned home.

A separate mobile army surgical hospital (MASH) existed at Lai Khe that had real doctors and nurses, the whole setup made familiar by the popular TV program and accompanying movie. Each division prepared its replacements for field duty in different ways. The 1st Infantry Division had decided that for newbie medics a week's stay at the surgical hospital simply observing the endless train of wounded GIs and ARVNs, who had suffered mainly from booby-trap injuries, would suffice. The idea was to get you used to the sight of blood and gore. It worked. The hospital was set up in a large tent, or series of tents, and resembled an assembly line. Once the wounded either stabilized or died, they were sent to a real hospital for recuperation, in the one case, or the division morgue, in the other, to be processed for shipment back to the States.

A Battery, 2/33 Artillery, 1st Infantry Division.

Sufficiently inured to the sight of blood, I hopped a ride on a supply convoy for A Battery, 2/33 Artillery, located at FSB Thunder II. Our battery consisted of six 105-mm howitzers arranged in a star pattern, with the sixth gun in the center. Each gun had a crew of seven to service it. In the event of a ground attack, which, as mentioned, had happened the week before I came on board, the center gun would shoot parachute flares straight up to illuminate the area while the remaining guns would level their barrels in order to fire either white phosphorous rounds or fléchette canisters, the equivalent of Civil War grapeshot, at the onrushing enemy. A circular wall of sandbags protected each gun, while a perimeter of barbed concertina wire and sandbagged fortifications enclosed and protected the fire base as a whole. Together with cooks and other support personnel, and also extra bodies for perimeter defense, the battery comprised about one hundred men in total. I was the sole medic on the base. Occasionally, various armored units that patrolled up and down Thunder Road would come into the compound to park their tanks and armored personnel carriers (APCs) for the night, but we were usually left to ourselves.

The retiring medic, "Doc" Martin, had reached the end of his tour and was scheduled for DEROS, the one acronym everyone in Vietnam knew and remembers to this day. It stood for date eligible for return from overseas. He stayed on a couple of days to help with the transition. He was very helpful and bequeathed his army medic's handbook to me, which I still have. Oddly enough, as I mentioned earlier, these were not standard issue, and until he gave me his I had never seen one before. It became my Bible and I always carried it in my medic's bag. The four months or so I spent at the battery, the guns fired more or less continuously either in support of infantry units in the field or in an exercise euphemistically referred to as reconning by fire. This meant that practically every night (when not otherwise engaged) the battery would pick out some arbitrary area of the surrounding jungle and shoot it up in the hope that they would catch a VC or NVA patrol unawares and do substantial harm. To convey some idea of how much ordnance was expended, the word came down one day that collectively the several batteries of the 1st Infantry Division had surpassed one million rounds. Just the financial cost of this was mind-boggling to contemplate. But because of the almost continual shooting, I had to deal with a lot of minor injuries caused by the handling of the ordnance and the recoil of the guns.

It is almost impossible to describe to someone who has no firsthand experience how loud the collective report of five 105-mm howitzers can be when fired in unison. During the dry season, the concussion wave thus occasioned would instantly cause a cloud of dust to spring into the air in a large circle around the guns. We were always hot and sweaty during the dry season, and many of the men went without shirts. The red dust clung to and coated their sweaty bodies with the effect that they begin to resemble the American Indians from the set of a Hollywood B-list Western. Although everyone had been issued earplugs, the concussion dust rendered them useless. The act of inserting and withdrawing them from your dust-coated ears would quickly rub your ears raw, so the earplugs were soon discarded as useless. Consequently, nearly everyone suffered hearing loss to one degree or another. I certainly did. I had bought a new Seiko watch before I left for Vietnam. Before my four-month stay in the battery I could hear it ticking; after the battery I could no longer do so, and I had trouble hearing certain frequencies, especially the higher ones—a disability that has remained with me the rest of my life and which now requires a hearing aid.

I had a lot of regular duties beside just waiting around for someone to get injured. My real job, as I quickly learned, was chief sanitation officer of the battery. Malaria was a real scourge in Vietnam at the time, and all troops were supposed to take a small pill daily called dapsone that was normally used to treat skin infections and leprosy but was found to be effective as a prophylactic for one of the two strains of malaria, *Plasmodium falciparum*. The other strain, *Plasmodium vivax*, required one very large horse pill to be taken once a week as a supplement to the daily little pill. It was one of my duties to stand at the mess tent every Friday and hand out the horse pill and make sure that everyone swallowed it. Another duty was to check our water trailer periodically to make sure the water was safe to drink. A hundred men can consume a lot of water, and for this purpose we had been given a water trailer that had to be filled daily from whatever pond or ditch that was nearby. One can imagine all the mosquito larvae, water buffalo dung, and mud with which it was contaminated. It took a lot of (chlorine) bleach before my tester would register "safe." Still, the cooks routinely boiled all water used for drinking, but it retained a horrible taste. The retiring medic, Doc Martin, had dutifully instructed me how to use the kit supplied for testing the water.

He also showed me how to burn the shit, the absolutely most revolting responsibility I had as chief sanitation person. A kind of outhouse had been erected at one end of the base. One sat on a board with a hole cut in it and defecated into a fifty-five-gallon drum that had been cut in two. When the drums had filled to about halfway, it was my job to drag them a safe distance away, pour in about five gallons of diesel fuel, stir it into the waste, and light them on fire, which produced black bellowing clouds of foul-smelling smoke, and if the wind shifted, enveloping the whole camp in a miasma of toxicity. A viler, nastier odor than burning diesel and feces does not exist. I am told that army personnel who performed this duty in Iraq qualify for a lifelong disability because the smoke was determined to be so toxic it produced permanent health effects.

These were my regular duties, but I did not have to wait long before I encountered my first serious casualty, a Vietnamese woman. Our FSB at the time (we relocated twice during my three-month stay with the battery) was located about a half a mile from a small village of maybe ten houses and several farm buildings—a ubiquitous feature of Vietnam. Every day a deuce-and-a-half truck assigned to the battery would haul the camp trash outside the wire to a dump. Several women from the village would wait patiently outside the gate for the trash truck and attempt to climb on to it and root through the trash for anything of value they could find before the truck discarded its load into a ditch. One of the women had slipped while trying to climb onto the side of the moving truck and fallen in such a way that her head fell under the rear tires. Like a ball, her head skidded free and avoided being squashed, but the weight of the tire crushed her shoulder and broke her arm, while the tread laid the skin on half her face bare to the bone. The driver threw her into the cab and rushed her back inside the wire and I was quickly summoned. I laid the skin back across her face and bandaged and taped it as best I could to stabilize it. I gave her morphine to alleviate the excruciating pain after determining she had no spinal injuries. Then I put her broken arm in a pneumatic splint and called for a dust-off chopper.

Barely a week later, another horrible accident occurred involving Vietnamese children. A gaggle of kids from the nearby village ranging in age from (probably) six to twelve were playing right outside the wire. One of them had apparently found a live grenade, or mortar round, which detonated, and suddenly there was a mass casualty situation. The call for medic went out and I rushed with my bag to find between twelve and fifteen wounded children in a classic triage situation. Triage is where you play God and are forced to judge who will die and who will not. You have to concentrate on those for whom immediate attention might mean the difference between life and death and ignore the rest. This is the circumstance I encountered. I called for a dust-off chopper and did the best I could. The chopper was there in fifteen minutes and another arrived very shortly thereafter to remove the remainder of the wounded and mangled children. How many doctors stateside in the course of their whole career would ever encounter a mass casualty situation like this? I venture to say very few. No wonder so many of the medics in Vietnam cracked. This was my real initiation into being a combat medic in Vietnam and the first of many situations that I encountered for which I was woefully unprepared. If I harbor one bitterness toward the army, not only for me personally but by extension for all medics, it was being thrust into life-and-death situations like this with such bare-bones training. I did the best I could with the meager training I had received, but the memory of those children, especially, still haunts me.

Casualties

Holding a sense of approach
has become crucial.
This has to do with time.
A prolonged waiting
can greatly refine this sense.

The black and fearful stench
of powder burned flesh,
torn and caked with blood,
will later be only a very close

and private education,
eluding sentiment or words.

The feeling as our legs grow tired
and vertigo sets in at the end
of a long and ugly hour before daybreak
is of helplessness, the delusions
of recognition and skill,
and of how all things return
to gratuitous surprise
and violence becomes the rule.

Several days later the dry blood
stain is a smear of soil
fading on the coat.
The people were in much pain, of course,
the short, frail bodies of the Vietnamese;
for many minutes the doctors compressed
the chest of one man,
trying to restore the life
motions of a heart that
insisted on staying dead.[5]

Aside from passing out malaria pills, monitoring the water, and burning the shit, I also acted as the resident doc for the battery, a service
all field medics were obligated to provide. The men would come to
me with all sorts of minor ailments, from colds to the runs, from skin
rashes to leeches and gonorrhea, universally referred to as "the clap."
I would usually prescribe two aspirins for anything with a fever and
an antibiotic ointment for the common skin rashes. In addition to these
standards, we carried Lomotil, a narcotic for diarrhea, and Robaxin,
a muscle relaxant for back pain. But not infrequently the men would
develop symptoms that were beyond my pay grade. Nearly everyone
in Vietnam, including me, came down at one time or another with a
so-called FUO (fever of undetermined origin), which had symptoms
that resembled malaria and often resulted in a very high, borderline
lethal fever, which required a stay in the hospital. Gonorrhea was the

most common STD (sexually transmitted disease) in Vietnam, and those who showed symptoms were routinely sent to the aid station in Lai Khe, where the medics administered penicillin, usually a quick cure for the disease, whether or not the patient was allergic to the drug. If they developed a reaction, the medics knew to quickly administer epinephrine to counter anaphylactic shock. My medic's bag also included a suture kit, though I never recall receiving any training in how to sew up a wound and do stitches. It turned out, however, that minor cuts and tears were a fairly routine injury for artillerymen since the violent recoil of the gun during firing often produced such wounds. Once again, I learned by doing. The thing I remember the most is how tough human skin is when poked with a threaded needle.

My first and most troublesome encounter with a superior in respect to being a 1-A-O CO occurred during my stay in the battery. It was the custom at our battery for the medic to share a bunker with the commanding officer, in this case one Captain W. The captain was very gung ho, especially about the artillery. He carried around a sign, which he always placed next to his bunker, that read, "Artillery lends dignity to what otherwise would be a vulgar brawl." It was a nice, catchy saying, but I had problems with it as one might imagine. Captain W. was RA (regular army) and had trained at an elite military school somewhere in the Deep South.

Captain W. and I did not hit it off. He was obviously bothered by my CO status and somewhat aggressively challenged me on more than one occasion to justify my position. At first I tried to politely deflect his questions, but when he kept it up and his questioning shifted from awkward to totally inappropriate, I told him straight-out that I had no requirement to justify my stance and that, henceforth, I would not respond to any further inquiries along these lines. I could see the anger in his face, but he had no choice but to accept, and he knew it. The next day, however, I was told that I would no longer have the pleasure of sharing a bunker with him, which was far and above the most comfortable appointed bunker at the FSB. From that point on I slept with my clothes on in a one-man underground bunker—really a hole in the ground with sandbags over the top supported by sheet metal—my improvised bed a stretcher, ready for any emergency. I remember the rats scurrying around and nibbling at my fingertips at night, presumably for the salt in the sweat on my hands. It was a filthy, nasty hole, but I preferred its privacy over the awkward luxury of the captain's bunker.

Basically, the senior NCOs were more interesting than the officers. We had little contact with officers above junior grade. The officers we did deal with, such as the aforementioned Captain W., were either what we derisively called "shake and bakes" (ROTC) or RAs. The former had gone through ROTC programs at their colleges, which helped to pay for their educations. The great majority of these, however, once they had discharged their military obligations, had no intention of making the army their career. Many were clueless and incompetent, despite their training. The RAs, on the other hand, had often attended prestigious military academies and intended to make a career of the army. They realized they needed to make a name for themselves in Vietnam if they were to advance and further their careers. Consequently, they were all spit and shine and had more on the ball, militarily speaking, but whether the one or the other, they were nearly all junior officers—that is, captain or below—who were all the same age as me, give or take a year or two. None had previous experience of war. For the senior NCOs, with whom we did have daily interaction, the situation was radically different. They were older, many veterans of World War II and Korea. They were experienced and knew the ropes in a way that only comes with time. Consequently, they were often the real power behind the scenes, and even junior officers were wary of crossing or challenging their de facto authority and status.

Our senior NCO at the battery, termed the Chief of Smoke, was a case in point. Sgt. Dee was Filipino by birth. He had joined the American army as a teenager in World War II and fought in many hard battles throughout the war. After the war he became a citizen and made a career of the army. Vietnam was his third war—he had also served in Korea—and he was now on his second or third tour. Tough as nails, he brooked no nonsense and ran the battery with an iron hand and supreme confidence, which everybody respected, including the officers. One episode stands out clearly in my mind. The battery had been ordered to pull stakes and set up in a new location along Thunder Road. It was quite an operation to shut down, pack everything up, and ready it to be hauled by Chinook helicopters to the new site. The guns, for instance, were suspended in giant nets, slung from the bottom of the choppers. Everything else had to be packed up and loaded inside their bellies or put on trucks. The new site had already been cleared by bulldozers, with a berm thrown up around the perimeter. Everything else had to be done by hand by us: bunkers dug out of the ground and fortified, sandbags filled for the gun emplacements, concertina barbed wire unrolled and staked around the perimeter, mess and command tents erected and sandbagged.

From start to finish, there was no rest. In the heat and dust, we worked around the clock for thirty-six hours until the fortifications were complete. I remember people dropping like flies from heat cramps and dehydration. I pitched in with the hard labor but was also kept busy passing out salt tablets and making sure everyone drank enough water. One of the draftees decided he had reached his limit and sat down and refused to fill another sandbag. The corporal in charge reported him to Sgt. Dee, who quickly appeared. The sergeant ordered the soldier to get up and continue with the work like everyone else. He refused, saying he was exhausted and couldn't continue until he got some rest. Without a further word, the sergeant grabbed him, slapped him around, and then knocked him down to the ground. He then told him to get up, quit shamming, and get to work. Wide-eyed and incredulous, the young draftee got up and got to work. It was an interesting situation to reflect upon. Very few Americans, I came to believe, had ever been driven to the real limits of human endurance, and they mistook mere fatigue for total exhaustion. Sgt. Dee knew otherwise from experience and found such "whining" intolerable.

For a while I kept a journal, which was very important to me. Except for my friendship with Bill—and we were only stationed together for the last four months of our tours of duty—I was always conscious that I was an odd bird who had to learn to keep company with himself. This is not to say that I was not affable or sociable with my fellow soldiers. I enjoyed casual conversation and gladly participated in things like the daily volleyball game, our chief source of entertainment. But other than Bill, I never found another soulmate while in Vietnam, someone for whom I felt affinity at a deep level, and so I kept company with myself and my journal, which became my ersatz soulmate.

It came as a real blow, then, when after several months and toward the end of my stay at the battery, I lost it. The grief was real, and it came about in this way: Periodically I had to hop a ride to Lai Khe to replenish my drugs and bandages. Usually this required an overnight stay, since it was not possible to do the roundtrip in one day. The rear-area aid station had a bunker with extra beds to accommodate medics for just this purpose. After one of these restocking trips, I hitched a ride back on a solitary jeep heading for somewhere farther up the road from my battery. This was not a smart thing to do. Most vehicles drove in convoys protected by either APCs or overhead support—safety in numbers. Solitary vehicles invited trouble, and this is exactly what happened. At some point someone started taking potshots at us and the driver of the jeep gunned it as fast as he could, causing the jeep to buck and lurch and occasionally go airborne on the rough, rutted, potholed dirt Thunder Road. The Vietnam-era jeeps were notoriously unstable, and the driver probably endangered us more than the sniper by his panicked getaway. In the process my box of replacement drugs and my journal went flying, and, needless to say, turning around to retrieve either was out of the question.

On another trip back to the rear-area aid station, I had an adventure that involved two Sioux Indians from North Dakota. Like previous resupply trips, I was forced to spend the night at the aid station. Having reequipped and with nothing else to do, I made my way to the local enlisted men's (EM) club, which was nothing but a tin shack with sandbags about waist high and screen wire from there up to the tin roof. There would always be music of some kind droning in the background. Here one could order beer—usually San Miguel, a Philippine beer—and, if lucky, a pizza. For some reason I ended up sitting at a table with a couple of grunts in from the field who were from the Sioux Reservation in the Dakotas. One was named White Lightning and the other Eagle Feather, and both descended from a long line of famous warriors—or so they said. Both were serving with C Troop, 1st Squadron, 4th Cavalry, which traced its lineage back to campaigns against the Sioux before and after the Civil War, and so it was theoretically possible that their warrior ancestors had fought against the very unit to which they were now attached. They laughed this off as an odd quirk of fate, seemingly oblivious to the multiple layers of irony inherent in this. Eagle Feather, especially, looked as if straight off the canvas of Karl Bodmer or George Catlin: powerfully built, aquiline nose, piercing gaze. But the most interesting part was that all the two seemed to want to talk about was how they hated the Blackfeet, who, they quickly informed me, were the hereditary enemies of the Sioux. That this ancient and hereditary hostility should outweigh the catalog of injustices that could be uniting all Native Americans in a common cause struck me as very curious, especially because this was a period of growing political awareness and activism on the part of Native Americans—activism that culminated in 1973 in a violent confrontation between the FBI and the Sioux near Wounded Knee, South Dakota.

I sat and listened, spellbound, as we continued to drink round after round of beer. At some point Eagle Feather produced some pills and encouraged us each to take one. I never knew what it was, but for me it was too much. My head started swimming and I excused myself, but I never made it back to my bunker. I passed out in a small ditch somewhere along the way next to a rubber tree. Only after I came to the next morning and stumbled into the aid station with a ferocious hangover did I discover that I had missed out on beaucoup excitement that had occurred during the night as I lay passed out. The base had come under rocket attack, and one rocket had detonated close enough to the aid station to leave some ragged holes in the tin roof and to embed several pieces of shrapnel in the furniture. I removed one particular wicked and jagged chunk from the desk and have kept it as a memento. But, like I said, even though I was there physically, I have no recollection of the episode thanks to my newfound American Indian friends, but it did make for a humorous, though not particularly edifying, war story.

During my four months or so at the battery, we never experienced a ground attack as had happened the week prior to my arrival. However, mortar and rocket attacks were a fairly routine occurrence. In the case of mortars, one could usually hear the tell-tale *thump-thump* of the mortar rounds being fired off well before they landed, giving one time to make a mad dash for the nearest bunker and safety. The afternoon volleyball game was a major source of recreation at the base that everyone looked forward to. But on more than one occasion, the game was interrupted by such an attack, and it was almost comical to see everyone scrambling for cover. Such attacks seemingly transformed even the overweight and clumsy into good athletes.

On a couple of occasions, however, Military Intelligence put the battery under high alert for a possible ground attack. On one such occasion, which occurred at night, the army rolled out its impressive array of firepower as a prophylactic. The five guns were levelled and loaded with Willy-Peter (white phosphorous) rounds that had timers that caused them to explode just outside the wire, spraying anything or anybody that happened to be there with the burning phosphorous. The center gun was pointed straight up in the air and began firing off illumination flares attached to parachutes. These flares are incredibly bright, turning the whole area practically to daylight. As if that weren't enough, Cobra gunships soon appeared, outfitted with miniguns, and flew around the perimeter, spewing six thousand rounds per minute straight down into the surrounding jungle, the rate of red fire so great that the tracers (every fifth round) created the impression of one solid stream of fire accompanied by a tremendous roar. It was a memorable display, more impressive than any stateside fireworks show I ever witnessed. All I could think of was who thought up all these horrendous devices to kill our fellow human beings, and what did it all cost, especially since, as it turned out, the threat of ground attack was a false alarm. The army must have spent a million dollars on wasted ordnance alone that night, and the net effect was a few dead rats and snakes unfortunate enough to be lurking around on the outskirts of the base.

Camp Dogs

Somewhere above our closer spheres
the weights and motions of the air
have changed. The day is slate
and dull pewter, tired plans.
The season grows weary and now rests
cooler beneath the rain that's not quite rain,
between buildings and the passageways
of mud and wood-planked walks, roofs of tin.
Spotted and sick with yellow streams
the banana plants wait for us to leave.
Various and cunning dogs lie about
meditating on broken boards,
networks of passageways
and bunkers falling to decay.
At times they cease their games
and calmly at the fall of day
approach us with their dialogues.
The dogs choose to syllogize.
Their system is reasonably sound,
and canine ethics
in such uncertain times
are quite above reproach.
They speak of mutability
and how the vacant buildings lean
and break, futility of a fence,
where competition and anxiety
in wretched fields have lost all sense.

The dogs are strangely sad
to see us leave,
though we could not prevail
against the mastery of rats
and rain and unhistoric time.
Health, the humble hounds suggest,
and treasure some slight ignorance
toward a day when you may
no longer beat such foolish fears
on your own dark hearts.[6]

A month or so after I had settled in at the artillery battery, I discovered
Bill Clamurro had landed a position as the medic for a tank company
in the neighboring 25th Infantry Division operating out of Tay Ninh,
close to the Cambodian border. Although in different divisions, we
wound up in the same general area of Vietnam and, as the crow flies,
less than thirty miles apart. Though our paths never crossed during this
stage of our tours, we were able to communicate fairy regularly by mail

Bill in base camp.

from this point on. We also established contact with Andrew Phelan and a couple of the other political 1-A-0s from basic training.

With only a brief interlude as a rear-area clerk, Bill would spend the next several months out in the field as senior medic for Bravo Company, 2/34th Armored. The mission of the tanks was to support the so-called Rome plows, which were, in effect, monster bulldozers manufactured especially for the army in Rome, Georgia, hence the name. The dozers needed protection as they went about systematically laying waste to vast areas of previously pristine and virgin triple canopy jungle, their activity, occasioned by the American war effort, so emblematic of the massive ecological destruction that paralleled the human destruction.

Bill's reputation quickly spread, not only as a first-class medic but also as a unique personality. The article reproduced below, which appeared in the division newsletter, *Tropical Lightning News*, in October 1970, helped to spread Bill's reputation:

Dau Tieng. Take one-part comedian, add some poetry, season with medical training, and you have quite a unique individual known to his 25th Division buddies as "Groucho." He is Specialist 4 William H. Clamurro of Nutley, N.J., a senior aidman of Bravo Company, 2nd Battalion, 34th Armored. Nicknamed Groucho because of his resemblance to the famous comedian, Groucho Marx, and because of his ever-present cigar, he has brought a sense of levity to the serious job of conducting war.

Grimy tankers form lines to tell Clamurro of their ailments, such is the renown of his medical knowledge. But after one long and particularly elaborate list of symptoms from a loquacious patient, he finally told the man "to take two aspirin and call me in the morning." There is a serious side to the man, however. He has obtained a master's degree in English literature form the University of Washington and taught at the graduate level there. He also corresponds regularly with American poet Archibald MacLeish, who was his mentor for his four years at Amherst College. He has had poetry published in the Upstart at Princeton University, the literary magazine at

Bill on tank.

Amherst and the University of Massachusetts. A conscientious objector, Groucho is armed only with a medical aidbag and an ever-present book. He is looked upon by Bravo members as a very competent medic whose main prescription for their woes is a heavy dose of humor tempered by a spot of medicine.[7]

Chapter 4

Things We Saw on the Ground

(*Clamurro*)

The following eight episodes or scenes are what I saw or dealt with during the fourteen months that I was in South Vietnam, which is to say from December 7, 1969, to February 17, 1971. I was mainly attached to only two units: first, the 2/34th Armored Battalion (a tank unit), part of the 25th Division, and then the 15th Medical Battalion of the 1st Air Cavalry. I saw many other things more grim or revealing than what I mention here. But these events do reflect something of the texture of my experience during this time. As I've pointed out elsewhere, I was extremely lucky to have been in those two units, given that I tended to be more protected from the most harsh and violent contact of the direct encounters that many soldiers endured, and I was further fortunate not to have been the victim of any accidents or friendly fire. But in addition, the sense that I try to convey here is that, given my good luck in the times and places of my service plus the nature of the work as a medic, I had the advantage or privilege of being a kind of observer. What I saw on these particular occasions prompted me to think about the conundrums and frequent absurdities of this war.

Dead Puppy

It was mid-December, approaching Christmas, and I had only newly arrived in-country. After a brief orientation at division headquarters in Cu Chi, I was sent to Tay Ninh, my first assignment, the 2nd Battalion of the 34th Armored, which was a tank battalion.

Instead of being sent out to the field as a new medic usually would be for his first six months, I was at the base camp. They wanted me to organize and clean up the aid station's office records. They knew that I had a college degree, and so they thought I could do it. Base camp activity was easy, routine, even boring: sick call, pain pills, immunization booster shots, antibiotic injections for VD (venereal disease). But some of the men in the unit had found and been playing with a small puppy. It acted strangely, and then it died. Though not sure, we suspected that it was rabid. We had to find out.

My superiors tasked me to take the dead puppy by helicopter—packed in ice in a sealed canister—to the lab in Long Binh. After delivering the dog carcass to the lab techs, one of the NCOs invited me to stay overnight. And it was really too late to turn around and fly right back to Tay Ninh.

Long Binh was another world. The buildings were air-conditioned, unlike in Tay Nin. And these facilities were large, solid, and substantial, unlike the crude and flimsy huts of my battalion. Because of the holidays, the medical officers and NCOs were partying: good steaks, Scotch, pornographic films—proper American holiday fare. For me, at least, it was briefly a welcome change.

But I didn't forget about the dog.

Results back from the lab indicated that the puppy in fact was rabid. Back in Tay Ninh I had to give the two men who had contact with the dog—Finch and Duncan—the old, rather primitive anti-rabies treatment. Every day for a couple of weeks I had to insert a needle, as gently as I could, at the proper angle into each man's abdomen as he lay on his back. Each day the needle was to be inserted in a different place—I kept a record—the entry points finally tracing a circle.

I couldn't really know their pain, the sting of needle into this sensitive area of flesh. But they were strong, tough to the challenge. Finch's belly was smooth and a bit fat. This was to his advantage. Duncan was a lot younger, much thinner, and it made me worry. I kept hoping I could find the least painful spot, and do it as gently as possible.

The treatment ended and the two men were safe.

It was a strange ministry that I'd been called upon to do—a procedure for which I'd not really been adequately trained. This happened toward the end of 1969 and into the start of the crucial year of 1970. The invasion of Cambodia would happen in a few weeks. Our tank battalion would only be involved for a short time; as usual, the tanks got bogged down in the jungle and had to be withdrawn.

But something about the incident and challenge, the imposed task of transporting the dead puppy—the pain and absurdity of the whole incident—haunts me. It was what I had to do as a quickly trained, new, and barely competent medic. Was it a symbol or reflection of the bizarre and unpredictable reality of simply being here? And the paradox of being a medic—surrounded by violence, aware of trauma, injury, illness, and death, while at the same time trying to administer medical help and use the most sensitive, pain-avoiding touch.

The medic so often deals with the "after" and so many things that he may never be able to fully feel. We are closely, intimately there, but how much can we ever know?

* * *

The Rome Plow

Rome plows are monstrous, huge and purposely destructive machines. Like hulking, oversized snowplows, the massive blade is really an immense knife. The lower leading edge of the blade is sharpened, and as the plows push forward, they cut and knock down trees, bushes, and everything else in their path.

Their purpose was to clear the jungle away from the sides of the laterite dirt roads, as if to remove the cover of foliage that might possibly

Rome plows, *The Hurricane*, publication of Field Forces Vietnam, no. 25,
September 1970, private collection.

be used by enemy snipers. It was another method of defoliation—not
the devastating and deadly, poisonous Agent Orange, but still another
brutally destructive and ultimately futile tactic in a war that would not
be won. In this phase it was not directly a battle with the human enemy
but rather a war upon the earth itself.

At this point of my time in country as a noncombatant medic, I was
with the 2/34th Armored Battalion. The heavy and powerfully armed
tanks—anachronistic throwbacks to other times and places, to land
wars in Europe—were of little value in a land of jungles, rice paddies,
uncertain fields, and an enemy whose strategy and very nature were
built on a conflict largely without a conventional front or massed
armored forces.

So the Rome plows were smashing their way through the forest,
felling and uprooting everything in the path of their enormous blades.
The tanks followed along behind as best they could, struggling over

the wreckage of what had been jungle. I was on top of one of the tanks, behind the turret as always, a medic waiting for any need that might arise. We were there, I suppose, to provide protection for the Rome Plows, these roaring behemoths that probably needed little protection. Our purpose here was obvious and routine, but it was also strangely absurd and superfluous. Perched on the tank, I held on as it jolted and struggled over the wreckage, a chaos of tree trunks, broken branches, bushes, and leaves.

Over the flat back part of the tank a large spider—round bodied and almost the size of a baseball—crawled slowly, mindlessly, like any such creature, but almost as if dazed and confused at the catastrophic violence, his jungle world suddenly uprooted. Somehow he managed to crawl across the lurching surface of the tank, and he finally dropped off into the broken remains of the jungle.

This plowing down of the forest continued through a long, hot day. And at the end we returned to our base. What the Rome Plows had been tasked to do had been done. I really did nothing. My duties or service as a medic were not needed on this day. Fortunately. But as I surveyed the vast destruction, I was truly astounded at the immense size and power of the plows, their wide swath of destruction, the violence to the land and plant life, to the animal habitat. I could only sense the ultimate folly and futility of the whole process.

The Rome Plows lumbered across and tried to clear the land by destroying the forest and its life. And the waste of it all was the story of their massive blades.

* * *

The Death of Billy Caldwell

It was early April 1970. The tank battalion had been moved temporarily south from Tay Ninh to a place nicknamed Bear Cat. It was more than a little eerie. There were no protective bunkers, no sand-bagged hooches (barracks). My aid station was just a flimsy, unprotected tent. But nearby was a unit of the Thai army, and it was rumored that the Thais had a tacit agreement with the VC. For this reason the area—including the American forces—would never come under rocket or mortar attack. Or so it was hoped. I was apprehensive. Without bunkers or even an enclosing wall of sandbags, in this mere tent we felt vulnerable, almost naked. But soon it came to feel normal, a strange illusion of safety taken for granted.

One of the other medics, Timo, was originally from Finland. Previously conscripted into the Finnish military, after he came to the United States, he was drafted again, into our army. Timo was rather rigid, stuffy, and authoritarian. I found all of this a bit droll. We were, for now, base-camp medics. In the small and poorly equipped tent we dealt with routine sick calls, minor ailments, booster shot injections, and skin-disease problems. Mainly it was quiet and at times tedious. We wondered why we'd been deployed here. Increasingly the war seemed unreal and far away.

One night I was asleep on my cot in the aid station tent when suddenly a frantic guy from the communication center came running over and roused me from my sleep. "Hurry up!" he said. "There's been an accident at the motor pool. One guy was killed; one's been injured!"

I scrambled into my clothes, still dazed—it seemed like the middle of the night and more like a nightmare than full consciousness— grabbed my aid bag (needlessly), and got into the ambulance jeep and drove to the motor pool. I was still dazed. The tank motor pool was in darkness except for a few lights near the scene of the accident. By the time I drove up, it had all been over for at least for forty minutes. The injured man wasn't really injured, but he was rather shaken emotionally. The dead man, however, was definitely dead, his body crushed beneath the track of a huge VTR (a tank "wrecker" or retrieval vehicle).

He had been sleeping on his cot in the open air and probably never awoke to the reality of his own destruction. He was covered with a blanket amid the wreckage of his cot. People stood around, bewildered. I took the stretcher off the jeep and, with the help of two other men, loaded the body onto it and put the litter with his corpse on the rack. The boy was nineteen. He had been a tall, well-built blond guy.

I think that I remember talking with him once. He had struck me as agreeable and pleasant. But now his body was an inert, brutal weight, his face ashen and covered with dust. We took him to 133rd Medical Detachment, a clearing station very close to the motor pool. We told the man on night watch to call one of the doctors to pronounce him dead, then we brought in the litter and placed it on the floor of the room. Slowly blood began to drip off the end of the litter by his head, pooling on the floor. The night CQ (charge of quarters responsibilities) neatly folded a light-blue cloth under the trickling blood.

I got back into the jeep and drove the body to Graves Registration, the unit that did the official identification of any corpse and prepared the body for return to the States. The men there were waiting. They had seen it all before, so many times.

It was somehow possible for me to do it all—though I didn't really do very much—and do it without feeling much of anything. I wasn't fully awake, or perhaps aware. I could not have been. Thoughts, realizations, sentiments came to me later—after the body had been dealt with. Later in the day, I almost broke down. But the actual image, the dead body, had no one single effect that I could identify—which is to say, no coherent effect. Perhaps the event had an element of significance or initiation for me. I can't say. The particular death in question was absurd, senseless, and pathetic.

There would be an investigation. Perhaps heads would roll up in the command. But the horror would not be undone.

His name was Billy Caldwell.

The next morning at roll call formation, Caldwell's death was mentioned. There were regrets expressed but nothing ceremonial. It was just another misfortune. While standing in the formation, another soldier, one of the regular tankers, turned discreetly toward me and said, "I don't know how you could have done that. I couldn't have." He was referring to my taking charge of Caldwell's corpse.

I didn't say anything in reply. I had done nothing special. It was just my job. There would be for me many more such tasks. But I couldn't help thinking, "You guys have the jobs of killing people, and yet you are squeamish about handling a dead body?" It seemed to me to be a weird detachment or disconnection. After the morning formation we all returned to our routines, but not as if nothing had happened.

* * *

"Doc! Doc!"

It was night, after-duty hours back at the base in Tay Ninh, and I was off duty. I was in the EM club having a beer and a somewhat mediocre pizza. A panicked and visibly upset soldier rushed up to me and blurted out, "Doc, Doc, you gotta look at my dick!"

I looked up and said, "I'm off duty. You can come to the aid station tomorrow morning during sick call hours." But the man was insistent, truly frantic, and he wouldn't take no for an answer: "No, no, Doc! You have to look at it right now!"

"Okay," I told him. With weary resignation and truly without enthusiasm, I suggested that we go to the latrine for needed privacy. This was not my idea of a pleasant or relaxing off-duty break. The man revealed the source of his alarm. It did look rather bad, a venereal chancre that would frighten anyone. I kept a calm, detached attitude, and I reassured him that at tomorrow's sick call the real doctor (the medical officer, not a mere corpsman) would take care of the problem and that all would be well.

To my almost surprised relief, the man immediately calmed down. He seemed largely reassured. And it was as if just my inspection of his infected member and my simple expression of a more or less comforting opinion had been enough.

It was more than a little strange. I was only a crudely and superficially trained medic. I was not a physician, a real doctor. And yet so often the men came to me with their diseases, confusions, and complaints. They made me a kind of reluctant but necessary authority figure. It was as if my rank or my role were enough to satisfy their need in moments of uncertainty and panic.

In this particular and somewhat lurid case, the frantic soldier reminds me of a simple and familiar fact: war is not just about killing and death, wounds, fear, and dreadful accidents. It is also about sexual license and ill-advised physical actions. Men at war almost always become men at sex. In the past the contracting of an STD was considered by the army to be "line of duty no." But with Vietnam it had become "line of duty yes," meaning that soldiers could and would be treated without any negative stigma or punishment, even without any criticism.

It was wryly and almost bitterly amusing: as a medic at the base-camp aid station, a very large part of my activity during sick call each day involved the administration of antibiotics to the men who had contracted gonorrhea or various other STDs. It was almost comical. In a way, the removing of any stigma or demerit for STDs seemed to have made the men casual and careless about sexual activities in a general way. And this carelessness, plus the knowledge that they would be treated for any disease, had the unfortunate effect of encouraging some men to return to dangerous behavior again and again. In some cases, however, the strength and persistence of the infection intensified. Some of the infected, returning after several cases, found that the usual dosage of penicillin or other antibiotics no longer worked, and in these cases, they had to go on to a higher level of medical treatment.

But what of my own role and identity? Did I really contribute to healing? Was mine a positive role? The suspicion haunted me, the sense that I inadvertently provided a kind of support, some level of reassurance or a slight restoration of confidence. I was not qualified to really do what had to be done. Nor was my limited knowledge truly adequate to the task. Barely trained but authorized as a medical corpsman, I was inescapably invested with the aura of knowledge and capability that I really did not possess but that the other men needed.

All of the US Army medics, especially in Vietnam, included those who were there in the thick of things, in the field, but also some who would have to deal with the aftermath back at a clearing station. We had to see, look after, and deal with the sick, the wounded, and inevitably the dead. In the paradox of our role and the fact of distance or presence, we were both separate from the inflicting of violence and simultaneously even more intimately involved with its results. The 1-A-O noncombatant medic would see this with special perspective.

* * *

Standing Down

When the tank battalion—2/34th Armored of the 25th Division— had to stand down, the division being withdrawn from Vietnam and sent back to Hawaii, we had to basically dismantle our unit, the aid station, and whatever was left of our supplies. There were many still-useful things left over—bandages, sterile syringes, medications, pills of all sorts. They could not be shipped back to the States. I asked my superiors if we could simply give them away, donate them to a local Vietnamese doctor or a clinic. They told me that, no, we couldn't give away any of this still-new, usable material to the local Vietnamese doctors or clinics. What must we do?

We were ordered to destroy it all. There were some large, empty fifty-gallon oil drums, and so we poured in diesel fuel, ignited it, and tossed in all the unused medicines and medical equipment. One by one we threw in unused sterile syringes, bandages, and pills. There was no orderly accounting for anything. It was just a wholesale discarding of material that, when it was originally procured, was quite valuable and that even now would have been usable. It was an absurd action, wasteful and perverse. But it also could be seen to reflect and symbolize much of the larger endeavor that was our presence and our project here in this jungle of confusion and futility.

In dismantling the 2/34th Aid Station, however, I found other things that didn't fall under the classification of the medical supplies that we are ordered to destroy. I took the office's dictionary. Many years later I would write a poem about this old book.

Old Dictionary

I have so many dictionaries, English, of course,
and bilingual, Spanish-English, likewise

those for German, French, Italian. Books
I do not read, page after page, but rather

consult to find meanings, an equivalence,
or how to spell a word, correct a memory.
But this old Webster's is a special case,
traveled with me to so many places,

shelved and opened for more than forty years.
On its cover is written in black ink
2/34 Aid Station, but even without
this crude mark I can't forget that when

our tank battalion stood down and I
was reassigned, Vietnam, 1970, I took
it, perhaps illegally. I couldn't bear to leave
it be discarded, yet another piece of trash,

our brutal residue. Though just a well
worn book, it links my lost identity,
a conscience, and so many dead.

It was not really clear to me why I wanted to keep a mere book.
Dictionaries are useful, of course. But there could have been other
reasons why I decided to keep the book. While I was in Vietnam,
I found myself voraciously reading as many books as I could get my
hands on. Friends back in the United States sent me books, and there
were sometimes random shipments of cheap books (paperbacks) that
arrived and were provided to the troops. Some people may imagine
that a war zone is nearly always in a state of great activity or tension,
built up as we prepare for combat—or later that we are in some condition of exhaustion in the aftermath of some battle or violent encounter.
But as often as not, and in fact very often, it was the tedium of waiting
and of routine duties. This was especially so for medics, not just those
back at the base camp but also those out in the field.

And so for a good deal of my time there in Vietnam, I had done
a lot of reading. I suppose that, in part, it was a kind of escapism,

a welcome distraction from the reality that we could not escape. The struggle against boredom was, for many of the soldiers, especially the youngest, very hard. For many of the soldiers this fight with base-camp boredom led to the abuse of drugs and alcohol. This should not be surprising. In any case, I had my own personal aid in my own struggle: voracious reading and a little booze. This dictionary became a memento that would stay with me for many years.

* * *

Withdrawal

In a later assignment, toward the last months of my tour, and when the 25th Division had been withdrawn, the men with remaining time in-country having been reassigned, I was sent to the 15th Medical Battalion, 1st Air Cavalry, in Phuoc Vinh. It was a clearing station. This means that, aside from routine medical service for the men at the base camp, it received the wounded directly from the field, usually brought in by medevac helicopter, and the doctors provided immediate emergency aid before the most seriously injured men were transferred to the more fully equipped hospital facilities near Saigon. But this unit also had wards where the sick and less gravely wounded men were taken care of.

It also had a unit for a kind of rehabilitation for those soldiers who, suffering from the effects of drug addiction, had turned themselves in, in hopes of getting some adequate treatment. Unfortunately, the only method used in this so-called detoxification program was simply the discontinuance of any drugs—going cold turkey. For me this often proved to be a frustration, a true problem.

I was on night duty one evening, and for the most part all was quiet. It was, as always, boring, and I tried to read or otherwise distract and keep myself awake, as was required for my night-watch duties. At one point a soldier walked in, a stocky African American. He had been in the drug rehab ward, and he was now sweating profusely, trembling, barely able to walk or speak coherently. I realized immediately that he was going through severe withdrawal. The symptoms were obvious and distressing. He pleaded for help. But of course I'd had no training on the proper medical assistance, no knowledge of what I could and could not give him. So I grabbed the phone and called the officer (I'll call him Major R.) who was in charge of the drug rehab unit. I explained to him what was going on, how the soldier was in acute, horrible distress.

I asked the major what I could do or give this man. The major told me that I was not allowed to give the man anything. I pleaded with him, but he said no. The soldier could not be given any medication. In effect he would have to "sweat it out." There was nothing that I could do or say, really. I helped the man back to his cot in the ward. He would go on suffering. It struck me as a harsh act of cruelty. But perhaps the clearing station had nothing really effective or appropriate for such cases. And yet I couldn't help but find this deeply wrong.

The next day the major came in and dealt with the man and with the others in his situation of drug dependency or withdrawal. I never found out what became of this particular soldier.

Wars are about suffering, of course, many kinds of suffering. But wars are also about drugs, the drugs that we in the medical unit are required and allowed to administer for pain and for other legitimate needs. This particular war was also about the drugs—illegal and powerful—that the men took to enter into altered states, whether for escape or unwise recreation it is hard to say. I came to realize that Vietnam was as much about varieties of drug usage as it was about a violent and murky military conflict. It was troubling. Sometimes in my hooch I'd all but stumble over a man hunched over, sitting by the wall, on the floor, in a semiconscious state. A friend of his told me that, well, he'll only do it while he's here, in-country. When he gets home he'll stop. Drugs won't be as cheap or readily available. I was astonished at this absurd assertion. As if the man could get off his addiction as simply and easily as he would get off the plane that brought him back to the United States.

As I looked around at this pervasive and strange situation of so many kinds and usages of drugs—the permitted ones that I and other medics dispensed and the supposedly illegal drugs that so many soldiers were using—I was struck by the bad luck or bad judgment of these men, but also by the twisted logic of it all. We were fighting in a confusing and absurd, incomprehensible conflict, and it was taking place in a part of the world notorious for its rich and varied abundance of drugs—opium, marijuana, and much else. For many addiction may be almost inevitable; and withdrawal, in more than one sense, may end up being a necessary and unavoidable suffering.

* * *

Body Bag

It was also in this last assignment that I dealt with what was one of my most grim tasks. As I mentioned previously, once again I was serving as an all-purpose medic at the 15th Medical Battalion clearing station. Given my level of education and previous experience with the 2/34th Armored Battalion, I was assigned to be the A & D (admissions and dispositions) clerk. What this meant was that, in addition to the obvious and routine duties of a medic, I was the one who took care of the records for the battalion, things like the names and conditions of those brought in, who was admitted to the ward, and also the first attempt at identifying the bodies of the soldiers killed in action. The cadavers were brought here in black vinyl body bags. They were conveyed by ambulance jeep or by helicopter and were usually placed right outside the backdoor area of the clearing station. When a corpse arrived, I was notified and went outside—with clipboard, ballpoint pen, and documents—to where the bag had been laid on the ground.

It was my task to unzip the large black bag and search through the effects and remains of the man. I would look for his dog tags, for a wallet with identification cards of any sort, for whatever could give his name. The dog tag would also have his serial number and his religion. When I was able to determine the religion as well as the man's name, I immediately contacted the appropriate army chaplain. When I couldn't find the religion information, I'd call the Roman Catholic chaplain, just to be sure to give a solemn final word.

This part of my role at 15th Medical was tough. The dead brought to us in the body bags were often in states of extreme mutilation, not having died neatly or peacefully. This was a war. In some cases the contents of the body bag included not only the violently killed and disfigured corpse but also much of the muck and vegetation of the jungle, scooped up and thrown along with the cadaver into the bag. It was as if the man's death had not just happened and been brought here to be identified, but that it was a manifestation of the place, moment, and brutal horror of his sudden death. The contortions of the slain body and the filth of the jungle where he fell powerfully told the horrific story.

On at least one occasion, such a horribly mutilated corpse arrived with much of the jungle also thrown into the body bag. I did my best of find the dog tags or other identification, but I couldn't find what I needed. The body would be sent on to Graves Registration, where they had better methods of identification and where the body would be prepared for being sent home. But in this case, and without success in finding his religious affiliation, I called the Catholic priest. When he arrived and I opened the bag for him, the priest was visibly stunned, shaken. He offered the proper prayers and I closed the bag. The chaplain then turned to me and said, "I hope that he died quickly, did not suffer too much." I nodded in agreement. But who could know? The dead man's final moments—whatever really happened, his suffering, consciousness, or unconsciousness—would all be a secret story. The grief would be for his family and others, far away. For me and for other medics here and elsewhere, there would be many more body bags.

* * *

Cu Chi: A Retrospective

Cu Chi was the division headquarters for the 25th Infantry Division of which the 2/34th Armored Battalion was a part. And so while I was usually stationed with the tank unit in Tay Ninh, somewhat northwest of Cu Chi, I often had to go down to division headquarters on one or another sort of business.

As an aside, the profound historical irony of Cu Chi as a major US military camp should be mentioned. As my 1-A-O medic colleague and good friend Jim Kearney likes to point out, Cu Chi provides an apt symbol of American ignorance and folly in the Vietnam misadventure given that, even as we were invading Cambodia in 1970 to find and destroy the VC (or NVA) command center, that very same command center was hidden under our feet (the US Army totally unaware), deep in the famous Cu Chi tunnels—now a favorite tourist stop for American veterans and others visiting Vietnam.

Once on a brief visit to Cu Chi, probably in June of 1970, I ran into another 1-A-O medic, Ramos, who had been with me in our basic training company at Fort Sam Houston in the summer of 1969. Ramos was one of the new soldiers who was from Puerto Rico, and while Puerto Rican citizens could not vote in US elections, they nonetheless could be drafted. During our training at Fort Sam Houston, because Ramos did not know English well at that point, I often had to do a quick translation into Spanish, since I knew that language pretty well. It was a pure coincidence that this young man from the same training unit a year before was now in the same division as I was, though in a different battalion.

On that June 1970 visit, Ramos told me about the death of another basic training classmate, Robert Childress. Ramos said, "Childress se murió." (Childress died.) He had been in a grunt unit and had been killed by a booby trap. I was deeply upset. Childress, a brilliant and personable, deeply religious African American youth had greatly impressed all of us by his seriousness and gentleness. He was outstanding. Later (starting in June of 1970) I had to write a poem in his memory:

Letter to R. C., Killed 12 May 1970

> I met you in the midst
> of one harsh summer
> when the roses burned
> on their weathered stems.

Behind your jokes
and all the other words
you told me of your death;
and I ignored all this,
the weight of inexorable time.
One day you were killed
and I will not understand.
We knew in that summer
that you were ill-intended
for this place; you tried
to tell us your time was short.
And one day the sun rose
on a wide green forest
and a thread of highway
awaiting the rain;
I met a vague shared friend
and the letter. I spilled
a few weak words
of protest and disbelief.
Somewhere you had died,
will die, and you are dying still.
Later I will hope to find
it had been a mistake
and see you in a hundred halls,
in strange hospitals.
Until I see that it is not you,
that the terse words of the letter
were not false.
And imagination crumbles
as I recall
how I failed to listen
as you told me of this,
of this future that had held the fact
and endless repeating of your single death.[1]

This sad news that I got from Ramos on June of 1970 was further compounded by the grim fact that, several weeks later, I learned that Ramos also had been killed in the field. These dreadful events were back then inescapably powerful: these two fine young men—like so many others, but also from that unique and noble, fragile cohort of the unarmed 1-A-O medics—gave their lives. And in the totality of American sacrifice and human losses during the war in Vietnam, there were many, many more—most of whom were not 1-A-O medics, of course—who were tragically cut down too soon in their lives. But those who faced and accepted the particular and perhaps baffling challenge of going there to serve but without weapons suggests now, much later, a complex and lingering question of moral choice and commitment.

Chapter 5

Cu Chi and Cambodia
(*Kearney*)

The great majority of draftees who saw service in Vietnam stayed with the division and unit to which they were first assigned, from beginning to end. However, neither Bill nor I followed this pattern, as Bill alludes to in the previous chapter. My stay in Vietnam fell into three more or less equally spaced intervals of four to five months spent in three separate divisions: the 1st Infantry Division (Big Red One) based at Lai Khe, the 25th Infantry Division (Tropical Lightning) based at Cu Chi, and the 1st Air Cavalry (Yellow Dogs) based at Phuoc Vinh. My assignments also varied widely, which was also outside the norm. In addition to the artillery duty along Thunder Road, I was briefly attached to convoys supporting combat units in Cambodia, served a stint as a surgical hospital orderly, did fieldwork with a medical civic outreach project (MEDCAP) unit to treat Vietnamese for minor infections and ailments in Cu Chi, and ended up as a flight medic on medevac at Phuoc Vinh. Both in respect to geography and job description, I then concluded my tour of duty with a broader experience of Vietnam than the average draftee.

The reason for the transfer from the 1st Infantry Division to the 25th Infantry Division headquartered at Cu Chi had to do with the politics of the war. In January 1970 President Richard Nixon and National Security Advisor Henry Kissinger announced the first draw-down of US troops in Vietnam, which was part of their grand new strategy of the carrot and the stick: the carrot being the reduction of American presence in Vietnam and concomitant Vietnamization of the war, the stick being the unrestrained use of American air power along with the invasion and interdiction of NVA and VC sanctuaries in Cambodia and Laos. As luck would have it, the Big Red One, my division, was the first to be recalled, or, to use the preferred army parlance, to stand down.

The exact mechanics of these stand-downs never became clear to me. All I know is that I went through the process twice, and both times I received reassignment within Vietnam. From that I concluded that most EMs, who for the most part were draftees, did not get to follow the colors back to the States and, instead, were reassigned to other divisions. This, if my assessment is correct, was a smart thing to do politically because it made it look to the American public as if the war were winding down favorably, but it also reduced drastically the need for replacement draftees, which, when all is said and done, was the mainspring driving student unrest on the campuses across the country. I was reassigned to the 25th Infantry Division, which was the other large military component sharing responsibility for III Corps.

Because of the stand-down, the 25th found itself temporarily flooded with personnel for which it had no immediate use, and this was the case for medics like me. I was assigned a cot in a hooch with a motley assortment of other transferees with many different MOSs. Every morning we lined up and the sergeant in charge would read a list of menial tasks and jobs from around the base for which we would either volunteer or be assigned to perform. For the first week, for instance, I was assigned to a detail that helped unload supplies at one of the mess halls, but this generally only took an hour or so, leaving lots of free time. Technically, my understanding was that I could have

Cu Chi base camp.

refused this service, that it was the right of a 1-A-O to refuse any job other than that of a medic, but I chose not to make an issue of it. I was also assigned guard duty one night in a perimeter bunker, a curious assignment to say the least. Being 1-A-O in a wartime situation often put you in uncomfortable situations that by their very nature tested your convictions. The sergeant in charge of this detail, to whom I was asked to report, was astonished when I dutifully showed up without a weapon, and even more astonished when I refused the offer of one. He shrugged his shoulders in disbelief but accepted the situation, and so I sat alone in my bunker all night peering into the heavy darkness on the lookout for a VC sapper with no means to resist him should he appear. It was a long night.

To take advantage of my free time, I signed up to take both French and Vietnamese language courses that met for a couple of hours every day, a nice service provided by the base but attended mainly by officers. The Vietnamese woman who taught both courses riveted my attention from the first moment I laid eyes on her because she seemed to be the living embodiment of Phuong, the beautiful but enigmatic Vietnamese lady in Graham Greene's classic novel, *The Quiet American*, which I had recently read. My language courses and infatuation with my Vietnamese instructor, however, were soon cut short as the Cambodia invasion began April 29, 1970, only a few weeks after my transfer to the new division.

The invasion was the linchpin to the Nixon-Kissinger two-pronged strategy of US withdrawal and increased Vietnamization of the war. It was a big gamble that probably would have paid off had the combined ARVN and American forces succeeded in trapping and destroying the Central Office for South Vietnam, known by the acronym COSVN, which had set up headquarters in several large bunker complexes just across the Cambodian border from Tay Ninh Province. The invasion began with an assault by ARVN forces against the southern complex just south of the border contour known as the Dog's Face.

The North Vietnamese, however, had caught wind of the impending invasion and managed to escape by the skin of their teeth after an epic retreat through the jungles and a running battle of several weeks' duration to safer sanctuaries in northeastern Cambodia and southern Laos. Although there were pitched battles enough during the roughly two-month event, the North Vietnamese had made the strategic decision to withdraw and retrench rather than stand and fight. The result was that when the smoke cleared, the US and ARVN forces succeeded in capturing mountains of war matériel, destroying the three large bunker complexes, and significantly disrupting and frustrating the NVA, but the bulk of the NVA leadership and forces successfully escaped to regroup and fight another day.

The invasion was also a bombshell for the domestic antiwar movement as symbolized first and foremost by the Kent State tragedy, when the Ohio National Guard fired on unarmed students at Kent State University on May 4, 1970, killing four and wounding nine others.[1] Campuses across the country erupted in outrage and dismay, while the so-called silent majority rallied in support of Nixon to stage mass counterprotests in many American cities, principally in New York City by construction workers. This much is indisputable: the invasion threw gas on the domestic cultural wars, and what had been smoldering now became a raging fire, with the Kent State massacre sending shock waves throughout the nation. But for those of us in Cambodia, there was no inkling of what had erupted stateside until weeks after the events.

Cu Chi served as one of the two main staging areas for the invasion, and the 25th Infantry Division participated as one of the three principal American units involved, the other two being the 1st Cavalry Division (Airmobile) and 11th Armored Cavalry Division. For the US Army the invasion was first and foremost a massive logistics puzzle. To support thousands of men and hundreds of pieces of equipment on the move is a formidable logistical problem, even with an existing infrastructure of roads and railroads in place. But when none of this exists, or exists only in bare-bones fashion, a formidable problem quickly becomes a nightmare. This problem was compounded since the army was given only two weeks' advance notice to plan for the invasion.

   This is what happened in Cambodia, and I got sucked into this logistical nightmare. With no advance notice, I was told to report ASAP to a certain E-5 sergeant at the local motor pool, a fellow draftee whose MOS I never determined. Assigned a deuce-and-a-half, the two of us—he as driver and I as convoy medic—joined a large and motley assemblage of trucks, jeeps, tanks, and armored vehicles headed for Cambodia. We followed Route 1, which was another old French highway that led from Cu Chi toward the large town of Tay Ninh. We bypassed Tay Ninh and headed almost due north to a hastily thrown-up supply hub known as Thien Ngon that had previously served as a remote airstrip for the 1st Cavalry. Several poetic names described the border with Cambodia, such as Parrot's Beak, Dog Face, and Fish Hook. Thien Ngon was located just to the north of the Dog's Face and across from NVA Base Camp 707, which, as it turned out, was mainly a large complex of warehouses skillfully concealed in the jungle. Our job, I soon learned, was to ferry supplies into Cambodia in support of the 2/27th Wolfhounds, a renowned infantry unit attached to the 25th Infantry Division, and to backhaul rice and weaponry they had captured. For this purpose the Rome plows had cleared a make-shift, single-lane road of roughly fourteen kilometers' length into Cambodia, to a point where the jungle gave way to cultivated fields and a more developed road system.

   For the next several weeks I made this trip back and forth into Cambodia almost every day, and every trip, it seemed, was an adventure. The whole time I was there I never figured out the chain of command. No one seemed to be directly over us. My tight-lipped companion, who hailed from the Bronx, was one stripe above me in rank and seemed to know what he was supposed to do, so I didn't ask a lot of questions. We were never assigned a tent or bunker to sleep in and had to scrounge for all our food, which consisted entirely of C rations, though these were easy enough to come by in abundance since there were pallets of them just sitting around. We learned to make little stoves by putting a small wad of C-4 explosive—the stuff that made claymore mines go bang—in a c-ration can with one side

Thien Ngon supply base on Cambodian border, May/June 1970.

cut out. If you just lit the stuff with a lighter or match it would burn nice and clean and heat one's can of Spam or Vienna sausages nicely, but with a blasting cap, it transformed into a powerful explosive. I had quickly packed a rain jacket, a so-called poncho liner—the standard army-issue nylon blanket—and one change of clothes in my duffle bag and that was it. We slept in our truck the whole time. When it wasn't raining, we would put sacks of captured rice in the bed of the truck for mattresses and then sleep quite comfortably under our poncho liners. When it rained we had to sleep in the cab of the truck as best we could, but at least we stayed dry.

Cambodia was my scariest Vietnam experience even though I was only there for a couple of weeks—or was it longer? Honestly, I lost track of the days and cannot say for sure how long it was. It was unrelentingly nerve-racking and often quite dangerous. Our daily journey was, on occasion, a crapshoot with death, a dangerous gauntlet through fourteen kilometers of jungle over the hastily improvised (or nonexistent) dirt/mud roads that had been quickly cleared by the enormous Rome plows. Practically every day there were snipers, mines, RPGs (rocket-propelled grenades), and casualties.

On one occasion (and as one example) the convoy emerged from the jungle into a series of clearings. The carcass of a huge M-48 Patton tank sat in the clearing, the victim of a land mine. The force of the blast had left the body of the tank intact but had completely stripped it of its undercarriage, including drive wheels and track, rendering it useless, so there it squatted, abandoned as a kind of lonely monument to the waste of war. The convoy on which I was serving as a medic consisted of a command APC in the lead and about ten deuce-and-a-half trucks ferrying supplies into the interior. My truck, luckily, was the second or third in the convoy.

We had not gone much more than a mile past the abandoned tank, its image still fresh in our minds, when an incredible explosion wracked the air. The NVA had allowed half the convoy to pass and then detonated a large mine that they had cleverly buried in the road during the night under the second truck behind me. The blast was so powerful that it completely ripped all the sheet metal from the truck, leaving nothing but a smoldering skeleton. Needless to say, all the

Following the lead APCs into Cambodia. *The Hurricane*, publication of Field Forces Vietnam, no. 25, September 1970, private collection.

personnel in the truck died instantly. Fearing an ambush, those of us in the front of the convoy gunned our trucks and made a run for it while those in the back made their way around the wreckage as best they could. I never learned if the bodies had been recovered.

While tragedy was not an unusual occurrence, some of my adventures had an amusing side. On one return trip along the same road we were told to keep a ten-meter interval for safety. The trucks were loaded down with tons of captured rice. To carry more rice, each truck had a standard one-axle trailer hitched to it. It was the transition season between the dry winter months and the summer monsoon. We had begun to experience brief and intense afternoon showers as the harbinger of the coming deluge, but the soil was still parched and dry, causing the convoy to kick up enormous clouds of billowing red dust that choked everybody in the convoy and rendered visibility at best difficult and at worst impossible.

The officer in charge had received intelligence of enemy activity and a possible ambush. Hence, the ten-meter interval and an accelerated clip for the whole convoy. The combination of the truncated gap, the quickened pace, and the reduced visibility proved disastrous. Every time the lead jeep slowed down or was forced to stop, the following trucks began a chain reaction of collisions, each truck plowing into the rear of the one before it or veering off the narrow path to avoid hitting the vehicle in front only to crash into stumps and other debris left over from the hastily thrown-up road. To my knowledge no one was seriously injured, but for the vehicles it became a destruction derby. If we had had an audience, as at a real stateside destruction derby, the people would have roared their approval at the unfolding spectacle in a fit of schadenfreude. We slammed into the trailer of the truck ahead just as another truck gave us a glancing blow from the side, which neatly ripped off the right-side fender and separated the door from our truck. On the next occasion, the truck behind us hit our trailer with enough force that it jammed the hitch assembly into the frame of our truck in such a way that the trailer could not be disconnected from the truck—a problem since the collision had also flattened one of the trailer tires. There was no thought, of course, of trying to fix it. We just continued.

With a ton of rice in the trailer, it did not take long for the flattened tire to disintegrate and peel off from the wheel. The trailer began to whip wildly and spew its cargo of captured rice sacks along the road. Still we pressed on. This, of course, was a great strain on the undercarriage of the trailer, so it wasn't long before the axle ripped free, leaving us in tow of a giant sled with an ever-diminishing supply of rice. And in the meantime, the general roughness of the road, exacerbated by the increased tempo, had caused our engine to partially separate from its motor mounts, producing a ferocious clattering and banging within the motor compartment. This is how we arrived in camp. I am sure it was an amusing sight for those witnessing our arrival.

Needless to say, the truck was a total wreck and we had to be assigned a new one that, in a day or two, we were obliged to abandon in a rice paddy, forsaken in the mud of Cambodia, victim of an ambush by the elements, as it were. The convoy had crossed the paddy earlier when it was perfectly dry on a foray to pick up captured

Unloading captured rice from a deuce-and-a-half.

enemy matériel. After crossing the open field, our path then took us through a patch of dense jungle, following a timeworn but narrow ox-cart trail. Suddenly the convoy was halted. A Loach (small reconnaissance helicopter) had spotted a contingent of NVA directly in front of us, headed our way. We were told to turn around ASAP and beat a hasty retreat.

Turning the trucks around in the narrow path proved to be challenging and took up valuable time. The enemy was approaching. Our position became dire when the heavens parted, and it began raining only like it can in the tropics. We made it out of the patch of jungle, but the open paddy, previously dry and hard, had morphed into an impossible quagmire. The smaller jeeps and the APCs could still function, but all of the deuce-and-a-half trucks became hopelessly mired, and because of the approaching enemy, there was not time for the APCs to pull them free. The order was given to abandon the trucks and climb onto the APCs. If the trucks were ever retrieved, I never found out. Just another day in Cambodia.

On this occasion we could not make it back to the base camp at Thien Ngon before nightfall, when the road shut down, and so had to pass the night in Cambodia as best we could. For security we attached ourselves to a unit that happened to be bivouacking along the road to spend the night. We camped at a hastily thrown-up supply dump at the edge of the jungle guarded by a platoon of infantry and several armored vehicles of various types. Muddy and wet, we found ourselves next to a mountain of captured NVA uniforms that had been unceremoniously dumped in a pile on the ground next to the road. My army issue blouse was so muddy and disgustingly filthy that I decided to exchange it temporarily for a dry and clean NVA shirt. Just at that moment, a Huey appeared out of nowhere and set down not fifty feet from the mountain of captured uniforms where I stood. Out popped none other than the commanding general of the 25th Infantry Division, impeccably attired and bemedaled in his neatly starched uniform. He made a beeline with his staff for the captured booty, no doubt to inspect firsthand this tangible proof of the success of the Cambodian invasion, the captured uniforms being a suitable substitute for the usual body count. I quickly jerked to attention and saluted the general, who took one look at me and my NVA blouse and just shook his head in dismay, refusing to return my salute. After a cursory inspection and a couple of photos, the general hastened back to his command bird and off he went. To be out of uniform while on duty is a serious offense, but to have an enemy uniform on—well, I was petrified, as you might imagine, fearing that I had committed an unpardonable faux pas for which I could be seriously reprimanded, or worse. It was alarming at the time, but humorous in retrospect.

War makes you do stupid things. One day my companion, who, as mentioned, was also my superior though only one grade above me, decided we needed to drive to Tay Ninh, the closest Vietnamese town from the Thien Ngon supply base that also had a large and established army base that included a motor pool and repair shops. Three of our eight rear tires on the deuce-and-a-half had gone flat, and there was no way to get them repaired at Thien Ngon. It was about a twenty-mile drive over a decent but very insecure road to our destination. Ambushes and command detonated mines—since Iraq called IEDs (improvised explosive devices)—were a daily occurrence along this road. To make a solo drive was a foolish undertaking, but the promise of a cold beer and a hot pizza at the EM club caused us to throw caution to the winds. Completely on our own, without authorization, we drove out of the base one morning and headed for Tay Ninh. The trip, as it turned out, was uneventful. While the tires were being repaired, we enjoyed our beer and pizza at the local EM club, then headed back to Thien Ngon while it was still sunlight. While on a medevac mission over the same road at a later date, I snapped a picture from the air of a destroyed deuce-and-a-half. I often say to myself, but for the grace of God, there were I.

Cambodia gave me, in a small way, some insight into the incredible, almost inhuman, stress of warfare experienced by soldiers on both sides during the World Wars. My experiences in no way approached what these soldiers had endured. Still, the daily runs into Cambodia, the constant fear of ambush, and the horrible scenes of death began to fill me with stress faster than my psyche was capable of dissipating it, and I realized that had it continued like this, at some point I would have popped, like an overfilled balloon. I never reached that point, and my weeks-long stay in Cambodia was nothing compared to the years-long tours of soldiers in the world wars, but still it gave me insight into the phenomenon known as shell shock.

Poem, 16 December 1970

Explosions and the dust have lain us waste.
Sickness and the blood spilled on the eye,
exhaustion before the hard yet saving sky
on nights where an hour of quiet takes the taste

of the shared and foreign miseries away
from our constant fearful waking touch.
Of these grim accidents we doubt that much
worse will soon return, and then the day

that follows mocks us for that futile plea
as a jeep and stretcher dripping blood,
torn flesh, the weakness of life's threads,
the child already dead will make us see

we're still the fools of hope and can't even lend
a mere breath to a life thrust to its end.[2]

Militarily speaking, the whole Cambodian invasion was a failure. It underscored that the ARVN was not quite equal to the NVA; indeed, its performance had been altogether disappointing. Although the army captured mountains of matériel and destroyed many large bunker complexes, COSVN escaped to regroup and fight another day. But to read the assessments of the generals at the time, one would come away thinking that it had been an unmitigated success, a decisive blow to the NVA in South Vietnam and a turning point to the war. I have among my documents several publications, including *The Hurricane*, a publication of the II Field Force in Vietnam. This particular issue, September 1970, was devoted entirely to the Cambodian invasion and featured a long interview with Lt. Gen. Michael S. Davison, overall commander of the II Field Force, which included both the 25th Infantry Division and the 1st Cavalry (Airmobile).

I spoke earlier about the military mentality and its tendency to reduce profoundly complicated situations—in this case a prolonged, complicated, and dreadful civil war—to simple terms that mirror the tidiness and simplicity of military life itself. The interview featured in *The Hurricane* is a superb example of this tendency. In the interview the general points out, in a tone of self-congratulation, various statistics such as the numbers of bombs dropped, the number of so-called communists killed, and the vast amounts of matériel captured, and he treats these as ipso facto proof of the success of the Vietnam War in general and the Cambodian invasion in particular, an opinion that time has shown to be wrong. Over against the general's assessment, I offer a short quote from the Buddhist monk Thich Nhat Hanh, written in 1967, that turned out to be right:

> President Johnson has repeatedly said that the United States stays in Vietnam only to protect South Vietnam from the invasions of the North Vietnamese and from the communist ... I do not know how the people of other countries think, but no Vietnamese peasant can understand these arguments. ... The majority of the peasants take little or no interest in the problems of communism or anti-communism. ... The more American troops sent to Vietnam, the more the anti-American forces led by the NLF [National Liberation Front] become successful. Anger and hatred rise in the minds of the peasants as they see their villages burned, their compatriots killed, their houses destroyed.[3]

Chapter 6

Cu Chi
R&R, Intensive Care, Morgue, and MEDCAP
(*Kearney*)

After Cambodia I returned to my barrack at Cu Chi and also back to the situation I had encountered before Cambodia—namely, an existence where I had no real job or purpose. My life took on a certain monotonous routine, and the days soon stretched into weeks. As I look back, I realize that this was the defining experience for the great majority of Americans who served in Vietnam. It had been eye-opening to realize that, at least in my experience, only somewhere between 10 and 20 percent of those deployed actually served in the field and saw combat, as both Bill and I had, where the fighting and dying took place—something unknown to me before deployment but a realization brought home forcibly by the enormous sizes of the army bases at Long Binh, Cu Chi, and elsewhere. Except for R&R (rest and recuperation), or an occasional weekend pass into nearby Saigon, many of the soldiers stationed at Cu Chi (and similar bases across the country) never set foot outside the wire.

Weekly mail call was the one thing I looked forward to at Cu Chi at this time. Vietnam was the last American war where the mail served as the sole meaningful connection to family and friends back in

Hooch life at Cu Chi, with my hero, Bertrand Russell, in poster.

"the world." We were allowed only one phone call back home during
our year's tour since all phone conversations had to go over a single
transpacific cable and the bandwidth was limited. For the weekly
routine of mail call, we formed up in front of the first sergeant's
hooch, and the sergeant read out, one by one, the names of those who
had received mail that week. To get a letter was an immediate boost in
morale; to not receive one, a disappointment that colored one's mood
until the next mail call. This was a weekly ritual known to millions
of soldiers up until the wars in Iraq, at which point new technolo-
gies made it possible for soldiers to maintain almost daily, real-time
contact with their families. Such a change.

The written letter was so important to my other buddy from basic
training and AIT in Texas, Andrew Phelan, that he named his own
book about Vietnam simply "Free," since postage was free for the
soldiers in Vietnam.[1] Interestingly, Andy constructed his book as a

juxtaposition of his Vietnam letters to family and friends back home in the world with Civil War letters written by his great-great uncle, accompanied by running commentary.

Although not as prolific as either Andy or Bill, I wrote and received my fair share of letters, and like Bill, I only recently discovered that most of what I had received in the way of correspondence survived. The letters were crammed in a couple of cardboard boxes tucked away in an old storage shed on the ranch, yellowed and full of silverfish, spiders, and other critters, but otherwise still intact. They mean nothing to anyone but me, but just thumbing through them revives the deep significance they once held. The few letters I received from my parents were perhaps the most difficult to reread because despite our disagreements, there were still genuine bonds of affection there. I had forgotten that.

Bill Clamurro, however, took the prize as the most prolific letter writer of the three of us. He carried on a prodigious daily correspondence with numerous friends, with parents and siblings, and also with his mentor from Amherst College, the renowned poet Archibald MacLeish. He did not make copies of these letters but discovered once we undertook this project that several of his friends, his parents, and MacLeish had preserved his letters. As both of us keep reminding ourselves, this project has become a kind of archeological dig into our own past lives. The portion of chapter 7 titled "Letters Home" will speak for itself in this regard.

"Were you inside or outside the wire during your tour in Vietnam?" Every soldier who served in Vietnam will instantly appreciate what this question references and will recognize the vulgar acronym REMF (rear-area motherfucker) used by those who were out in the field to refer to those stationed safely behind the wire. Day after tedious day with scarcely any time off, these (for the most part) draftees toiled and labored by day and night in the various workshops, motor pools, and supply warehouses, retiring to their hooches during their off time to self-segregate into cliques. The three main groups were the brothers (Blacks), the rednecks (rural, Southern whites), or the heads

Sunset at Cu Chi.

(hip, urban whites from all over). Each tuned in to their preferred music, be it soul, country, or rock, newly made possible by means of the ubiquitous Japanese portable radio / cassette recorders, available duty-free in every PX (army commissary) in the country. They would then anesthetize themselves with either beer or pot, both of which we quickly realized were ubiquitous features of Vietnam, their real enemy not the VC or the NVA but the monotonous tedium of everyday routine and the often self-destructive habits they adopted to counter it. Ever the loner, I was not comfortable with any of these groups. I was affable and sociable but could not fit in, and I suffered from my self-imposed isolation.

Night Collection

At this hour of evening
shifting, dissolving toward night
there is no single purpose
to the sky.
The clouds suggest
whatever tentatives of mind

are given them or lost
in shadows of the changing light.
The distant and formless
will have become
the ground of given thought.
Above the low and realized
gray textures of dark
wood buildings, metal roofs,
the thin strung wires
now hanging peacefully
in the cessation of wind.
This and the knowledge
of barbed wire barriers;
the roads of dust
become invisible.
In this half night horizon
the aircraft move
with their sounds and lights,
points of green and red,
drawing their coherent curves,
but small in this foreign sky.
Composition is asked without much hope
from the heedless span of dusk.
The watcher plagues with words,
his need to know, the core.
The elements of time
in motions of the clouds
defy the very terms
with which they seem to play,
indifferent to the known forms
of our bleak geography,
machines, the points of light,
broken wanderings of our sight.[2]

And it was here in rear-area barrack life that the cultural wars that
were setting cities ablaze in the States concentrated, as if in a crucible, to flavor and define the Vietnam experience for many hundreds
of thousands of draftees. Racism and racial tensions were especially

My hooch mates celebrating down time with pot at Cu Chi. Notice the
blown-up poster of marijuana in the background.

pronounced. Bill has taken a keen interest in the role of racism in
American society in general and was quite distressed by its many
manifestations he encountered in Vietnam.

The Black draftees, especially, preferred to stay by themselves,
developing elaborately choreographed hand-shaking rituals that
were very captivating to watch and that came to be known as the
dap. Many of the Black draftees also wore a plaited black wristband
symbolizing Black Power. They, of course, listened almost exclusively to Motown, R&B, and soul, but this music was so powerful
and infectious that it crossed over. I often wonder if the crossover
appeal that (say) Otis Redding or Solomon Burke enjoyed did not
hark back to the exposure that many white draftees experienced for
the first time in Vietnam.

For those draftees stationed inside the wire, the tension, distrust,
and even hatred between the lifers (long-time career soldiers), who

controlled and directed practically every aspect of daily life, and the draftees, who chafed under the constant supervision, was ever-present. The generational gap between the two was as wide and deep as the Grand Canyon. The utter inability to bridge the chasm in any meaningful way led, on more than one occasion, to violent outcomes, and the violence went both ways. The lifers could call the MPs (military police) on you with, as will be seen, deadly consequences, while the ready availability of all kinds of weaponry made it possible for the EMs to retaliate and, on not so rare an occasion, assassinate their tormenters, a practice known as fragging.

During my stay at Cu Chi, the tension between the two sides escalated to the point that both situations occurred: death of a draftee at the hands of the MPs and the fragging of a lifer by unknown parties. The death of the draftee took place in a neighboring hooch. I never really found out the exact cause of the original altercation between the draftee and a senior NCO lifer that precipitated the shooting.

Kearney's souvenirs from Cambodia: rusty AK-47, NVA officer's pith helmet, NVA shirt, and wanted poster for a senior VC official.

However, the word was it had to do with illegal drugs, providing a case in point of the army's attempt to crack down on illegal drugs even as it dispensed legal drugs on a scale hitherto unprecedented. The altercation, however, turned fatal as the result of an unregistered war trophy (i.e., souvenir).

But back to the tragic story: A draftee who had never seen service in the field had nevertheless managed to acquire an NVA officer's pistol as his souvenir, which he loved to display and often kept tucked into his belt while inside the hooch. Souvenirs, I suspect, have held fascination for soldiers since the Roman legions invaded Gaul. It is a strange psychological phenomenon, this instinct to collect some tangible memento of the enemy to show off at a later date when back safe among family and friends. But this memento— even though it was useless since rusty and minus cartridges that would fit—proved deadly.

This particular draftee was considered a smartass troublemaker by the lifers: a pothead, argumentative, nonconforming, and always close to the line between disagreeable and insubordinate. On this particular occasion, he had apparently crossed the line and the sergeant had summoned the MPs to have him thrown in the brig, pending disciplinary action. When they appeared and saw that he had a pistol, without a further word they shot and killed him. It was a shocking and profoundly disturbing turn of events to us all and a stark reminder that in the army during wartime, the lifers had life-and-death power over us. I often wondered how the army announced something like this to his parents at home.

The second situation was a fragging that occurred on base sometime after the shooting, but apparently completely unconnected to it. The intended victim (he luckily survived) was a rear-area medical administrative officer whose demeanor and behavior had obviously created serious enemies. Like most officers he had his own private hooch, which somebody had booby-trapped with a grenade and a trip wire—the preferred method of fragging. This episode, which sent shock waves through the whole base, coincided with a rash of anti-

A disgusted lifer in front of a graffiti-laced mail bin.

war graffiti that mysteriously appeared sprayed on numerous walls and buildings across the base, suggesting that there was more than one person involved, perhaps even an underground organization, connected to and coordinated with antiwar groups back in the States, dedicated to fomenting dissent and even revolt among the draftees.

I had nothing to do with any of these events but nonetheless fell under suspicion. Like I said, I felt like I had struck a bargain with the army, and I intended to hold up my side of the deal, which precluded any activities of this nature. I had insisted on my legal rights as a 1-A-O medic when tested, and we were all tested at one time or another, but I had never done anything that could be considered even remotely subversive. I had, however, made my thoughts and beliefs known to friends and family in letters written back home.

It came as a great surprise, then, when one day out of the blue two MPs approached me and told me to follow them. They refused to answer my questions as to why and stated tersely that I would find out soon enough. I was escorted into a room with folding tables set up in the form of a square, around which several officers and their aides sat. I was informed that I was to be questioned by Military Intelligence and the judge advocate's office about recent activities of a subversive nature around the base, that I would be sworn to tell the truth, and that a transcript of all questions and answers would be written down. I was familiar with the process, since it resembled what I had experienced back in Houston when first inducted into the army. Basically, they wanted to know if I was any way involved with the recent rash of antiwar graffiti that had appeared around the base. I should say up-front that they were apparently satisfied by my responses to their questions since I never heard another word from them, but what sobered me was how much they knew. They reminded me that I had attended the SDS convention in Austin in the spring of 1969 and had gotten a copy of Mao Zedong's Little Red Book and that I had participated in antiwar demonstrations while a student in Austin. They also pointed out that I had expressed antiwar senti-ments in my correspondence to family and friends, including my former roommate from Germany.

This last revelation, especially, stunned me. I still had the naïve belief that private mail was sacrosanct, and it was upsetting to be abruptly disabused of this notion. The interrogation became a personal revelation into how paranoid the army, and by extension, all national intelligence services, had become. Sitting before this panel, I was amazed to learn that Military Intelligence had compiled files on my activities, which were entirely peaceful in nature and osten-sibly protected by our Constitution, that predated my induction into the army. It also made me reflect on the strange situation that I had found myself in after graduation at Fort Sam Houston, where I alone among my classmates had received no orders and sat in limbo for two weeks before finally receiving my assignment. Could these things be connected? Had the army found themselves in a quandary about what to do with me, this suspect 1-A-O medic with a connection—albeit tenuous—to the detested SDS? I will never know the answer, but I still wonder.

The year-long tour of duty that was such a defining feature of the Vietnam experience included as a matter of policy a short in-country leave and a week-long R&R to another country. I never took in-country leave, but I did take the R&R. In a gesture of generosity, the army also provided a free plane ticket to one of the several authorized destinations for the out-of-country break. These destinations included Bangkok, Hawaii, Australia, Hong Kong, Manila, Penang, Taipei, and Kuala Lumpur (Singapore).

R&R became one of those waymarkers that all Vietnam veterans can relate to. It also opened up a wider window to that corner of the world for many draftees who would not otherwise have ever enjoyed the opportunity. Vietnam, therefore, had the potential at least—as all foreign wars do to a greater or lesser extent—of being enriching as well as degrading. In practice, however, the decision as to what destination to choose for one's R&R usually boiled down to where the best prostitutes were to be found, which underscores that war and sex are inseparable. With very few exceptions, organized warfare has been between groups of young men in the prime of their lives and at the height of their sexual virility. War is about fighting, dying, boredom, intense anxiety, and (historically) male bonding. But it is also about prolonged periods of forced abstinence and monastic frustration. Vietnam was no exception. The *recreation* part of R&R, therefore, was usually a euphemism for seeking release from such frustrations by a week of unrestrained sex.

I was not exempt from these considerations. A system had evolved—tacitly approved by local authorities and winked at by the US military—that attempted to straddle the fence between official disapproval and outright acceptance. Accordingly, upon arriving in the country chosen for R&R, one would engage a young lady of the night to be one's guide for the week. It was a contractual relationship often even negotiated in advance through agencies set up for that purpose with offices in Vietnam. In addition to providing sex, she would take you around to show you the tourist sites by day and the nightlife in the evenings. She would also receive kickbacks from the numerous nightclubs and tea rooms catering to the American servicemen on leave. So, seen from the young ladies' points of view, their job was to steer you into these venues and separate you from your hard-earned money in as many different ways as possible, a task they became very proficient at.

Sex was not the main reason I settled on Hong Kong; for that the preferred destination was Bangkok, Thailand, which enjoyed a reputation for the best girls and cheapest sex. Hong Kong was still a British protectorate at the time, a lingering anachronism of the colonial era. In consequence of the decades of British administration, it was by and large bilingual, which was reassuring. I also had read a lot about twentieth-century Chinese history, and, of course, Red China was actively supporting the North Vietnamese in the war. Mainland China was closed to American tourists at the time, so Hong Kong and Taipei, Taiwan, offered the closest thing to a China experience. Hong Kong was also a bustling duty-free hub of international commerce, a big consideration for those who wished to acquire high-end gadgets like (say) fancy cameras or the newest tape recorders, nearly all of which came from Japan and which carried hefty tariffs back in the States that could easily double the price. Hong Kong had hundreds of small mom-and-pop shops that specialized in these items and catered to thousands of businessmen and tourists from all over the world as well as the hundreds of US military personnel on leave. This also played into my decision because I had a laundry list of gadgets I wished to acquire.

I did go to a bar recommended to me with the idea of hiring a girl. When you go to one of these places, a girl will come sit down next to you. You buy her a tea and settle into a conversation. Pretty soon you get around to the subject at hand and negotiate a price. I went through these motions with a very attractive young lady and after a few rounds of expensive drinks—she sipping tea and I drinking beer—we headed back to my hotel room. But once there things began to fall apart. She began to bargain for a better deal. And suddenly I was overcome with the feeling that this whole arrangement was so mercenary, so devoid of anything resembling a genuine human interaction that it was impossible to continue. I gave her a good tip but asked her to leave, and after that first night, I was on my own. With most people understanding English and Hong Kong being a very safe place, this was not a problem.

From then on I kept company with myself, filling my days by wandering around the shops and markets, delighting for the first time in the many gastronomic wonders of authentic Chinese cuisine—as opposed to what passed for Chinese in Texas at the time—visiting several museums featuring oriental pottery and art, and signing on to one of the standard tours. This tour featured an excursion boat that cruised Victoria Bay, allowing a close of view of the iconic Chinese junks anchored by the hundreds in the harbor. Our boat ventured as close to the mainland as allowable, permitting a glimpse of the mysterious interior in the distance.

The excursion was also noteworthy because I was seated with an Australian couple for the noon meal. They dutifully made small talk, asking me where I was from and what my job was in Vietnam. When I expressed in no uncertain terms my disagreement with the war, their reaction was not quite what I expected. They turned stony-faced and clammed up. I could only guess why, but they obviously did not want to hear what I had to say. I fell silent and after lunch excused myself. But that conversation, such as it was, was the only meaningful exchange I had the whole week. It remains an unsettling memory for me. I had the need to talk, to unburden myself, but they were obviously not comfortable with my confessional.

Another enduring memory still gives a chuckle. The movie MASH—the 1970 film featuring the shenanigans of the doctors, nurses, and staff of a Korean War–era field hospital who maintain their collective sanity by a combination of incessant banter, unbridled sexuality, and general kookiness, behaviors that violated all norms of military propriety but which the army brass, generally portrayed as bumbling clowns in the movie, seemed incapable of suppressing—had just been released in Hong Kong. Naturally, as a combat medic on leave from Vietnam who had experienced firsthand mobile field hospitals in Vietnam, I was keen to see the movie. When I saw it advertised one day on the marquee of a large theater in the center of the city, I quickly bought my ticket and took a seat in a packed house for the afternoon matinee. What was amusing was that although the movie was in English, I could never follow the jokes. The audience apparently could read the Chinese subtitles quicker than the actors could actually speak their lines, and the whole theater would erupt in laughter just as the actors delivered the punch line, making it impossible to hear. But the movie for me was very poignant, and I remain strangely conflicted about it: happy to see the spotlight focused on something I had experienced directly, on the one hand, but bothered that a reality so filled with pain and suffering could be used as a backdrop for unbridled gallows humor, on the other. But, alas, such is the power of the American entertainment industry to shape public perceptions the world over.

I returned from R&R in Hong Kong with an expanded cultural appreciation of Asia but was still sexually frustrated. The thought of my life being snuffed out in this stupid war without ever experiencing a truly satisfying relationship with a member of the opposite sex was very destressing to me and was a constant preoccupation during my whole time in Vietnam.

Without any regular duties, I continued serving as a temporary fill-in, usually for soldiers on leave, for several different and completely unrelated jobs, each of which was eye-opening in its own way. In this capacity I worked for a couple of weeks as an orderly in the intensive care ward of the on-base hospital, filled in as jeep driver for a major in charge of the base morgue, and ventured outside of the wire on a couple of occasions on MEDCAP outreach programs.

The brief two-week assignment to the intensive care ward of the 12th Evacuation Hospital was a shock, but at least I did have some rudimentary training from AIT to fall back on for the tasks I was called on to perform. I changed sheets with the patient still in bed, managed the bed pans, monitored IVs, administered pills according to the chart, took temperatures, and reported any disturbing changes to the head nurse. But what a change from being a field medic outside the wire to serving as an orderly in intensive care. The antiseptic cleanliness of the hospital as compared to the filthy reality of medicine outside the wire was striking. My two strongest memories from my two-week stint in the hospital are of an officer awakening from anesthesia to realize he had lost both legs and one arm from a mine he had stepped on and of witnessing the moment of death of a young soldier who had contracted spinal meningitis. I have to say, I was glad when this duty came to an end.

Thereafter, I was assigned to be the aide and jeep driver for Major A., who was in charge of the base morgue. The major, not the sharpest tack on the base, was something of a bumbling clown, and apparently his assignment as head of the morgue was one of those dead-end assignments for officers of his caliber. Although easily in his fifties, he had never progressed beyond the rank of major but obviously had decided to stick it out until eligible for retirement. It was my first opportunity to observe up close the interaction between officers in Vietnam. I was shocked by the downright disdain and discourtesy shown by the junior officers toward their nominal superior, the hapless major. They would belittle him to his face in a way that caused me to cringe, but he was so diffident and unsure of himself that he would take it passively.

When soldiers were wasted (killed) in the field, they were placed inside a vinyl body bag with a long zipper to seal it up. They were referred to as line 1s, short for "killed in the line of duty." Choppers would then bring them back to the base-camp morgue. Here the orderlies on duty—sometimes but not always with a medical MOS—had the unpleasant duty of undressing the deceased; washing the body if intact or, if not, placing the various body parts in some semblance of a human shape; and, finally, recording and packaging any valuables such as rings or watches so these could be forwarded to the next of kin. Bill Clamurro has written of having to perform this unsavory task himself in his narrative, "The Things We Saw on the Ground."

The bodies were then placed in a cooler in preparation for being shipped back to the States, where they could be claimed by the families for proper burial. Fortunately, I never had to participate in this gruesome task. My job was simply to whisk the major around from one location to another on the base, and on one or two occasions to actually take him outside the wire.

It was on one of these trips that I had a firsthand experience with one of the notorious Vietnam Army jeeps with which the army had replaced the iconic World War II– and Korean-era Willys jeeps. We had always had jeeps on the ranch when I was growing up. Indeed, I learned to drive in our 1956 CJ-3B, which I still own. The new army jeeps were supposedly more advanced, but far from it on several scores. In fact they were downright dangerous, and eventually the army scrapped the whole lot of them. The dangerous thing was, if you took a corner too fast, the front wheels could fold under the vehicle resulting in a nasty, often fatal, rollover. That nearly happened to us on a trip outside the wire.

Driving the jeep as I had the old ranch jeeps, and expecting it to respond accordingly, I swerved rather abruptly to avoid a Vietnamese moped on the crowded dirt road that served as a main corridor between Cu Chi and Saigon. The jeep began its fatal maneuver but, luckily, I was able to correct before the wheel folded under. I often reflected that if the army had just bought jeeps off the lot—they were then still essentially the same as World War II vintage jeeps—they would have been better off.

My most moving memory, however, from my brief career as chauffeur to the hapless major was a quick visit to the morgue on the occasion of a particular line 1 casualty. The major had received notification that a young 2nd lieutenant, fresh from West Point and of a distinguished military family, and only a week or so in-country, had been killed on his first mission outside the wire and was being transported to the morgue. The major apparently felt that he had to personally oversee the preparation for the young man's final trip back home in a coffin. We arrived at about the same time as the body bag and remained to observe as the bag was unzipped and the lieutenant was placed on a table to be prepared for the cooler. He had been shot through the chest by a machine-gun round and death had been instantaneous. I was struck that his uniform was starched and his boots were polished. He, no doubt, had looked forward eagerly to his Vietnam service as a necessary initiation into a long and illustrious career following in the footsteps of his forefathers, but his career had ended abruptly, unexpectedly, even unfairly. The bullets in Vietnam, or any war for that matter, pay little attention to whom is deserving. There is nothing fair about death in war. "For whom the bell tolls" is arbitrary and the luck of the draw; that is, at least, how Bill and I interpreted it.

Cu Chi is now remembered chiefly for the vast underground system of tunnels built by the VC that remained undiscovered and unknown even though the giant army base was practically on top of the complex. My stay at Cu Chi connects to the tunnels in a harrowing way.

On occasion, as mentioned, I was detailed to do MEDCAP duty. MEDCAP was an outreach program and, to my mind, one of the more successful programs sponsored by the army to try to win over the hearts and minds of the Vietnamese people. Accordingly, local village leaders would be notified that army medics would be made available at a certain time and place to treat villagers for minor ailments such as infections and skin rashes. Most of these rural villagers had no access to medical care of any kind at this time, so even rudimentary care was a welcome gesture that received an enthusiastic response. During a typical outing, two of us would drive a cracker-box army ambulance, often of World War II vintage, to the appointed place, park, and set up shop. We usually did this unaccompanied by any kind of additional security because the area around the base was considered (mistakenly) to be completely pacified.

On this particular day, however, we took a wrong turn, and before we knew it we were out in the countryside and completely lost. We pulled into a farmstead to turn around—it was not possible to do so on the narrow road—and try to retrace our steps back to the base. Here we were, two unarmed medics in a clunky World War II vintage ambulance, completely alone and lost in the Vietnamese countryside outside of Cu Chi. We both noticed immediately that there was something strange about this farmstead. There was a thatched house, a well, and various outbuildings, but there was not a soul around. Even more unusual, there were no farm animals around either: no chickens, dogs, water buffalo, nothing. And everything was immaculately clean and orderly. A model farm without animals and without farmers. I got the distinct feeling, as the hair on my neck began to stand on end, that we had stumbled into a place where we did not belong, that there was real danger here, and that we needed to *di di mau* (make haste) as quickly as possible. We threw the clunky truck into reverse, wheeled around, and beat a hasty retreat, and were mightily relieved when we finally found the road back to the base.

It is a strange trait that humans share with many other animals, the ability to sense danger palpably without really knowing why. I remain convinced to this day that we had stumbled on to one of the secret entrances to the storied VC underground city, which was disguised as

Model Vietnamese farmstead near Cu Chi.

a farmstead, and that for a brief moment we had been in real peril of death or capture. Be that as it may, for me nothing is more emblematic of the disconnect between American rhetoric about Vietnam at the time and the true reality of the war as it existed in the countryside than the tunnel city at Cu Chi. The fact that I experienced a personal adventure connected to it, whether real or imagined, adds personal poignancy to this fact.

Chapter 7

Reports from the Field
Vietnam '69–'71
(*Clamurro*)

In the task of returning to my experiences in South Vietnam as a 1-A-O army medic, I have not only scoured back through my memory but also gone through as many written documents as I could find. There were the texts in my notebook that later were transcribed and became the more than thirty poems that, along with several written much later, were published in my book, *The Vietnam Type-script* (2018). But this was not enough, and in some ways even the poems could be considered a step away from the immediate reality of the experience.

Fortunately—starting right around 2017 and 2018—I came upon a stash of letters that I had written to family and friends from Vietnam. Then a bit later more letters that I had written—in this second case to my college classmate friend, Jack Hailey—came to light when Jack was going through many of his own old and long stored-away possessions. In this way, by a series of unexpected and yet truly lucky accidents, a good deal of the past documentary evidence and memory support from my Vietnam time all surfaced. In what follows I have pulled together selections from these two sets of letters, and in doing so I've tried to revive not so much what happened (the obvious and often grim events) but rather what I was thinking and how the events and sights of my limited and particular experience affected me. This revisiting of those documents, of course, also has resulted in a portrayal of my struggle to both report back to family and friends and, at the same time, protect them from as much anguish and worry as I could manage to do. This is, then, a document about documents.

Part I: Letters Home

In 2018, as I was moving from Kansas to Delaware, I found a box of letters that I had written to my parents, to other family members, and to a few friends, all of which had been dutifully saved, in most cases with their original envelopes. This rediscovery came as something of a jolt. It was yet another case of a broadly sweeping, perhaps unconsciously done suppression on my part. In addition, tucked among my own letters, were some other letters to me from a couple of friends and no less than six letters to me from Archibald MacLeish that dated from August 4, 1969. to September 22, 1970. The first three were sent when I was in the army but not yet in Vietnam, and the last four were sent to me while I was there. A seventh letter from Prof. MacLeish was written to my father, dated October 16, 1970. Though short it was an especially touching letter because of his kind words about me.

What does one do with one's own letters, written under unusual and fraught conditions, from a war zone to one's family? These letters— now being reread forty-eight years later—strike me as a peculiar mixture of the utterly trivial, mundane reports or checking in that a soldier would send to his or her parents, and at the same time as a strange combination of evasions and self-censoring meant to reassure and protect one's family from anything that might increase their anxiety. Any soldier's parents had to have been already under considerable emotional stress simply knowing that their son (me, in this case) was in a war zone. Moreover, the Vietnam War in that period from 1969 to

1971 was being given extraordinary attention by television and other news sources—which is to say, coverage of what was happening over there—while at the same time within the United States the war was a source of immense social and political uproar and conflict.

This being the case, what was a soldier in Vietnam to do? My parents knew that I was there, and I did give them some sketchy information of where I was located from time to time. I also reported, in carefully oblique ways, on what was going on. But it was always highly filtered. I could allude to one or another violent event, but it always had to be put at a distance, made vague and general. I down-played the reality of what I saw as much as possible. I also felt that I had to project an air of calm and say that I was well and that things in my immediate area were quiet, which was, in fact, often the case. Nonetheless, I did make some negative and critical comments and observations. I did, for instance, get more than a little political in my harsh views of what I saw or knew was going on in Vietnam at the time, especially during the period in 1970 when the so-called Cambodian invasion took place. But to a certain extent, as I now go back and reread, I find much of my reportage to be almost unreal and deliberately artificial.

I mostly painted a picture of my day-to-day life as a noncom-batant medic as one in which things were largely routine and tran-quil. As I reread I'm astounded at the prevalence of descriptors like *quiet, peaceful,* or even *boring.* The truth is that, yes, in the two units in which I served—first in a tank battalion and then in a medical battalion—and especially at those times when I was in a base camp, many of the days and nights were boring and uneventful. This was often a problem for many of the younger soldiers. The combination of tedium and confinement in the camp led to their attempts to escape through excessive use of drugs and alcohol. But at the same time, it was not peaceful in the state-side, civilian sense, because our phys-ical, geographical situation left us always vulnerable to the sudden violence of incoming rockets or mortar shells—which did indeed often cause damage, fear, and injury.

In any case, I have returned to my letters—lost but really just stored away for so many years and now recovered—and I've studied them in an effort to collate their now-strange contents with my also time-altered memory. The attempt that I offer here is another part of the project of rendering my own individual, personal (and thus subjective) limited experience. It is also a commentary on what I have elsewhere called the conscience that was lost. By that I mean the consequence of the discontinuance of that peculiar army classification, the 1-A-O noncombatant medic, of which I was a part and which, with the ending of the draft in 1973, came to a complete end.

This rereading of my own letters, unsurprisingly, underscores a sense that I had back then that I was a soldier with a peculiar and complicated status. First of all I was a medic like all the others, and second, I was a legally and specifically restricted noncombatant medic within the army. Finding myself in this identity, I was in more ways than one an observer, a man most of whose duties came after the fact, to aid and minister to others. In addition, some of us medics were often a bit away from the point of violent first contact. This was, for me at least, a defining part of my perspective.

Another feature of my role and situation while in Vietnam was, quite simply, the remarkable good luck of being in the two units to which I was assigned—first with the tank battalion and later with the 1st Air Cavalry's medical battalion at its clearing station. My locations within those units were usually somewhat protected or away from the thick of things. As a result I came through the whole experience of more than fourteen months with the good fortune of not merely surviving but also of not having been wounded or having contracted any one of the many common diseases that afflicted so many returning soldiers.

Of the letters themselves, those that were saved and stored come to a total of seventy-three. And although I arrived in South Vietnam on December 7, 1969, and left on February 17, 1971, my first letter (to have been saved) is dated January 5, 1970, and the last one is from

February 2, 1971. Many years later, in 2018, after going through the
collection, I wrote the following poem:

Letters Home

> Long tucked away in a small cardboard box,
> the year of letters that I wrote home
> to a mother and father who must have been
> gripped in an anxiety I could never share.
>
> And it was over me, for I was there
> in jungles of confusion, violence, and fear,
> the constant taste of its absurdity
> more than the dust and heat that I'd at first
> found unbearable but soon learned to bear,
>
> just like my job, to treat the sick and wounded.
> The imperative was to wait, to just endure.
> So I wrote home reporting some of what
> I saw, but cautious to filter out the worst,
>
> with fictions to protect them from the truth
> and hardness of that time and place.
> They kept my letters safe, and I forgot,
> so that reopened forty-eight years later,
>
> I see them as they quietly insist:
> "We are your war stories, evasions,
> incomplete. But now you must return
> to face and speak your life's truth one last time."

The basic slant in my letters, from the beginning, was to portray
my situation with a certain candor but also as calm and uneventful.
In my letter of January 7, 1970, I say in part that "I work fairly hard,
do my job efficiently and patiently; and I make an effort to stay on
people's 'good side'—mainly by staying out of their way. Otherwise,
things are quite quiet and even pleasant."

This last statement, though mostly honest, might well have struck my parents as less than fully accurate—or perhaps as not really credible. But there was in fact a good deal of routine and often tedious time in the base camp. Perhaps for this reason, in this initial period of my time in Vietnam, and all through my fourteen months, I consciously endeavored to read as many books as I could get my hands on. I also tried to write a lot—mainly notes that became poems, but also many letters. Now I realize that these activities were not only a way to confront the tedium but also were the response to a deeper need and were thus a strategy (of which I was not fully aware at the time) to save or protect myself from a full confrontation with my situation.

During this time I not only wrote poems and notes that later became finished poems and were even published, but I also carried on an intermittent but valuable correspondence with Archibald MacLeish, with whom I had studied creative writing when I was a student at Amherst College. In my letter of January 11, 1970, I mention having received a letter from MacLeish, and I mention that I am sending my parents some rough drafts of poems: "The enclosed poems aren't quite what I wanted to say, but one has to start somewhere. I guess I erred in the direction of excessive melodrama; things are hardly as disquieting, especially in recent days." The remark is partly honest and partly (maybe less than credibly) filtered, intended to be reassuring.

In a few places in the letters, I mention the awkward problems that we men of the 1-A-O medics classification presented to the expectations and norms of the military. In my letter of January 17 I talk about the conundrum of putting a 1-A-O medic on guard duty—an activity that, usually, all members of the battalion did from time to time, on a rotation basis. This gives rise to a sly comment on the play of semantics that so often arose. I note that "if the Command fears that 1-A-Os can't exactly be used as guards, they put us in the same place, behind the same M50 [machine gun] or booby-trap switches, but they call us not Guards but Forward Observers! I.e., call something a different name and [it] becomes different."

Not only legally but also technically as well, we 1-A-O medics never received any proper weapons training. Thus, putting one of us at a machine gun not only would have been illegal but also would have been irresponsible and dangerous. But this, once again, brings up the core question of who we were and what exactly we were doing in this situation. In other words, at many points in my time there—and the same was true for the other 1-A-O medics—our status and our training put us in a curious and awkward position. It also presented a strange and frustrating set of problems for our fellow soldiers and often for our commanders. Fortunately for me, in one instance a newly arrived staff sergeant saw this inappropriate use of men in my classification for guard duty and also realized that I was needed to staff the aid station office most of the time. So he took me off the guard duty roster. Looking back, it is interesting and significant to see how a simple, logical decision can be made, even if, for others in a military unit, there should not be any exceptions or adjustments.

Another important aspect of my gradual acculturation to the real nature and tendencies of the military was my increasing sense of the many types and levels of corruption that existed. I had no prior illusions about the ways in which things in any army or military organization functioned. I had always suspected that corners were cut and complete honesty was not the usual custom. As I wrote home in a letter of February 3, 1970, "I'm slowly getting to see and realize an amazingly corrupt system." In particular I mention the abuses done by supply personnel, things like black market activities and similar actions. But in the same letter I also note that "there is an unbelievable (maybe not) amount of 'racial friction.'" This mainly had to do with some, but not all, interactions between the white and the African American soldiers. It was more prevalent in some base camps than among soldiers out in the field, and there were memorable exceptions in which friendships between Black and white soldiers were sincere and strong. But along with the material corruption (e.g., in the supply operation and also in some cases of record keeping), this unfortunate state of human interaction was disappointing. The racial tensions, where they existed, could be seen as another sort of corruption or breakdown. Toward the end of that same letter I note that this corruption is "like rotten wood: everything you touch crumbles and proves to be basically worthless."

At a certain remove—both at the time, when one thinks of people "back home" getting one's letters, and much later when the writer himself, or someone else, reads old letters from a soldier to people back home—something about the reportage of the conditions in the field often appears less than candid. It seems unrealistic or improbable. But one of the basic and odd facts about the war that I saw and knew—and that I suspect many other soldiers experienced—was the peculiar extreme of certain paradoxes and stark differences. This is to say that, yes, a war is about violence: wounds, damage, and death. But it is also about rules, routines, often absurd commands and decisions. And very often more than anything else, it's about tedium. This was a severe problem in Vietnam at certain times and places, especially in the situation of base camps and the effect of the confinement and boredom that so many of the men had to endure.

As a medic, first of all, and because at age 24 I was already an "older man," many of the soldiers who came to sick call or consulted at other times seemed to have felt that I had some special level of knowledge or the resources that could alleviate their problems, some of which were not just physical. In a letter of March 16 I talk about this, first in a rather routine way, then touching on some more interesting challenges. There were the routine cases, "but also a lot of skin damage, severe sunburns, and (oddly enough) a number of more or less serious 'nervous conditions'—anxiety, depression, and/or hypertension. I've had to learn [or mal-learn] by experience the use of various strong sedatives ... I'm reluctant to use or give out any sort of strong calmative or depressant. Some of the things that cause such states of tension are too deep-seated to be treatable with these medicines ..." In effect, I and many other medics had to take on the role of counselor or psychological support. Once again, this fits in with what I've noted at the outset: the idea that a medic often comes in at the aftermath.

The medic—even if this view on the part of the other soldiers was not warranted or justified—was almost automatically accorded a level of respect and was assumed to have a degree of knowledge and skill that the other soldiers, in a moment of need, urgently required.

In the month of April 1970 and as we approached May, I sensed that something was brewing, and in fact we were on the verge of the Cambodian invasion. At this point my unit, the tank battalion, was back in Tay Ninh, which is very close to the Cambodian border. For this reason our unit could not be left out of the action. But as an armored (tank) unit, our participation had a built-in conundrum and problem: we had these powerfully armed machines and were close to the field of action, but at the same time, tanks proved to be—over and over again—highly inappropriate for movement and combat operations in the soft earth and tangled vegetation of the jungles. Largely for this reason—or so I assumed at the time—although some of our tanks participated in the initial invasion phase, our unit was withdrawn to Tay Ninh very soon after the incursion began.

I myself was, once again, extremely lucky because I was still assigned to the aid station at the main base camp; thus, I did not go with the field units that were involved with the invasion. But as I sensed the approach of this operation, and as it unfolded, I was something other than my normal calm self in what I wrote home. As ill-informed as I was about the particulars and the larger strategic or smaller on-the-ground facts of this operation, I nonetheless saw the whole thing as being a foolish, futile, and absurd yet highly indicative reflection of America's actions and conception of what we were doing.

And so in my letters I let my discipline and calm control slip. As we began this operation, I wrote on May 1, 1970, that "this present ensuing month of May looks like it brings a further & perhaps irreversible widening of the war; it may signal a slow-down in actual troop 'withdrawals,' & in general it has been a sort of low blow to the morale of the men & (I don't hesitate to admit) to mine." In the same letter I later add that "This 'noninvasion' of Cambodia is a pure and pragmatic military move; i.e., as far as military science goes, it may be a good idea, but it also displays Nixon's basic contempt for negotiation &/or compromise & his unconcern for the possibility of a bigger war, Chinese involvement & God-knows-what." In my next letter I become even more angry and harsh with regard to this move and toward Nixon. In one passage of the May 4 letter I bluntly state that "Bitterness & fear are the order of the day. And (for me) anger."

Like so many others, I really could not have predicted some of the consequences of the Cambodian invasion, but by the time of my next letter (May 5) the word of the four deaths at Kent State had come to our attention. Over and above being truly horrible and criminal, the Kent State killings were also yet another symptom and an inevitable consequence of the madness that simply was the US Army in Vietnam and the basic delusion of our government's view of the world. It was the strangest thing for many of us there in Vietnam at the time: here we were in a nominal war zone, and yet an incident of shooting violence was taking place on a university campus. It made no sense—and thus it was bitterly fitting for the larger picture: the corrosive chaos that our policies and actions in Vietnam were having created more chaos and violence within our own country.

There was no way that most of us—especially the soldiers in Vietnam itself—could have known at the time, but 1970 was a crucial and complex time for America's involvement in Vietnam. It was, supposedly, a continuation of the process of Vietnamization that Nixon had begun and that—especially for many of us conscripts there in the field—held out the hope of our withdrawal from harm's way. But at the same time there was the Cambodian invasion, which was later to prove tragic for Cambodia. Then, in early 1971, it was followed by the Laos incursion. Things would continue to deteriorate (e.g., the infamous 1972 Christmas bombing of North Vietnam, etc.) until the nominal ending of direct US military participation in 1973, and finally the collapse of the South Vietnam regime in April of 1975. But for those of us there on the ground, little or none of this could be clearly seen or understood.

Meanwhile, as I continue to go through my letters and piece together their now odd-seeming contents, and as I look into my own memories of that time, along with the sentiments that I had then and that partially come back to me now, I'm struck by the strange contradictions of what I experienced and then wrote. In a letter written on April 4 and before any solid sense of the upcoming Cambodian invasion, I say first, "Don't be fooled! The War & the so-called Vietnamization isn't going as well as Nixon and the US press would like you to believe: it's a thin fabric of apparent control, which is about to be rudely & brutally torn (if recent happenings in Laos & Cambodia are any indication)." Then a bit later in the same letter I state, "But I am for the most part enjoying my stay in Vietnam: I read, I talk to the various men, I tease the Vietnamese, & I continue my readings." This latter passage is both true and yet eerily implausible. I was doing the writing; I was trying to stay in touch and to reassure. And yet this sort of assertion must have struck my readers as evasive, if not bizarre.

An example of another sort of evasion comes in my letter of May 15, 1970. I state that "I got a little tired of my desk-job, so I opted to go out to the field; I'm in one of the less active, more secure (?) units: headquarters' company tanks. ... I am relieved to be away from the routines & pressures of daily, weekly & monthly reports." But in fact I had been feeling a bit harassed by one of my medic colleagues who I'd say was having certain psychological or mental problems. And so I basically quit the scene. Just a few lines later in the same letter, I once again stress the idea of peacefulness: "It's very quiet & pleasant here, thus far. I trust that the rest of my tour will be suitably sedate." Now I find myself wondering about both my own sentiments and motives at the time as well as my readers' reactions. Were these assertions crazy lies or sincere hopes?

For a brief time, at FSB Washington, things indeed were mostly tranquil and routine. But this was about to change abruptly and in a peculiar way that, once again, brought up the thorny issue of my identity as a 1-A-O noncombatant and the legal limitations on how I could be deployed. In the letter of May 20, as I find myself suddenly back from the field to the Tay Ninh base camp, I start one passage with a phrase that sounds like the start of a story: "A funny thing happened to me today; & I'm not sure yet how I feel about it." In effect, I was called back from FSB Washington. I relate the following:

> Today as I was innocently reading the Skin Disease book, my platoon Sgt. showed up & told me I had to come back to the battalion area in the base camp. The reason is that the present Awards Clerk is about to leave Vietnam (in 10 days) & the battalion is having a hard time finding a replacement, so I've been chosen to "fill-in" for a week or 2 until another clerk (with suitable qualifications) comes into the battalion. It's not a job that I want at all: it involves writing up award citation texts, &c., all day; it means working in the main S-I office, under the nose (as it were) of the bn commander & other such important folks; & mainly it would mean a thankless job which would have absolutely nothing to do with medicine. Also, it is illegal (i.e., "against Army regulations") for a medic to work out of his field like this.

It turned out that the excuse first given to me—that a real clerk would come soon—was not true; they wanted me more or less permanently in the awards clerk position because (alas for me) they knew that I had an MA in English. Ultimately, after a few short weeks I became aware of some embarrassing and possibly unethical irregularities in a few of the previous awards records. While this had nothing to do with my work in the short time that I'd been there, I simply did not want to be in that position if and when any of this came to light (perhaps it never did). And so I quit the job. When my superiors tried to pull rank and insist— or more charitably, simply tried to plead—that I stay on, I told them emphatically that I would complain to higher authorities (the inspector general's office), using my 1-A-O status and its legal limitations. At that point they agreed and let me go back out to the field.

This strange and awkward interlude as an awards clerk went from about May 20 to July 20, when I returned to another FSB. Things there were mostly routine and, believe it or not, uneventful. I believe that at this time there was at least one minor but revealing and distressing incident that I can recall. Since the FSB was by definition stationary and well equipped for us medics, from time to time men from a grunt unit would come to the aid tent for medical attention. One day a foot soldier came in to have me look at his case of ringworm infection. I was astonished: both of his legs were totally covered with ringworm. I said that he should immediately leave the field and get advanced medical attention. He replied that there was no way that he would be let go or excused from field duty. So he went back to his unit. I have no idea what happened after that. Ringworm is not a fatal affliction, but at the extent that this man had it, it would take a long time to cure, and might never completely be purged from his system.

Meanwhile, as August and September drew on, we had a noticeable sense that our battalion would soon be shutting down and that we'd be leaving Tay Ninh. But at about this time I was looking ahead to the end of my tour of duty and when and how it would end. If I simply chose to leave Vietnam at my twelve-month regular date, I would then still have five months or more of army duty back in the States, and this idea was not appealing. Alternatively, I could opt to extend my time in Vietnam for about two more months (thus into February of 1971) and as a result get the bonus of leaving the army completely upon my return to the States. And so this second option is what I chose to take.

In my letter of August 24 to my father, I break this news to him and my family. At this point I and the others in the 2/34 Armor Battalion are rather clearly seeing the upcoming stand-down, or removal of our unit from Vietnam, and so I sense that, when I'm reassigned to another unit, it will probably be to a medical battalion or some other similar place, one that will be safer, out of the field. I first mention that supposition to my dad: "The rest of my tour should be fairly sedate & in fact if the unit pulls out & I stay here, I stand a good chance of getting an interesting re-assignment, possibly to a Med. Battalion or to one of the evac hospitals of the 68th Med Group or to a flight dispensary, etc." This note was intended, I think, consciously or unconsciously, to both reassure my family and to rationalize my subsequent decision.

As I say a bit later in this quite long (four-page) letter, "The above impressions, and several other reasons which I will expand on here or in future letters, partly have prompted me in my decision to stay on in Vietnam for 70 days past 6 Dec. (until, that is, 14 Feb. '71) in order to ETS from the Army five months prior to 14 July '71."

In the very next paragraph, I have the perhaps insensitive nerve to understate the affair, knowing that my decision had to have been a terrible disappointment, if not an upsetting blow, to my family. As I too casually put it, "I realize that this tentative decision of mine may disappoint you all somewhat, since you had expected me to be home by December or earlier." I go on from there to express my general pessimism about my future in graduate school and even about whether I really want to go on, finish, and try to get a job in college-level teaching. Now as I reread this long letter, I see how it is simul-taneously low-key and evasive of any strong emotion and yet also suffused with a deep but veiled pessimism, both about myself and about the state of American culture and society. Why exactly I am so pessimistic and negative at this moment? Is it doubts about myself, or is it a grim, cynical view of our society? I cannot now remember or say. But there it is, written down in my own hand. As I say a bit later in the letter, "A lot of what I say reflects (maybe) the rather dim view I now have of the state of American society (especially some political, economic & ecological trends which I think I see); I feel that I'm a fairly loyal citizen, but I feel that there's little or nothing I can do to ameliorate a condition that seems to go from bad to worse." It could be argued—especially now, in 2018—that I have always tended to be negative, pessimistic, and a tad cynical. But I also suspect that my frustrating and eye-opening time in Vietnam had contributed to my sentiments and decisions in August of 1970.

Toward the end of this letter I again refer to, or excuse myself from, a decision that could only have been hurtful to my parents. In yet another case of clearly insensitive understatement I say that "I hope you don't mind too much my decision to extend." In retrospect I can barely believe that I could have been so casual and offhand about this decision, a drastic change in my calendar of my time in a war zone, and that I could have written like this to my family. Yet at the same time, this phrasing and the complex impulse behind it are in many ways honestly indicative of the inner turmoil and struggle of a person trying to announce and explain an upsetting decision and at the same time trying to project an air of confidence and reassurance. How does one successfully achieve or get to this impossible balance? Looking back on this and other such passages from a distance of nearly five decades, I'm struck by how my attempt to be calm about such a major decision probably came off as being deeply upsetting in spite of my desire to reassure.

For me the autumn of 1970 was a significant and interesting turning point. By October it was now clear to all of us in the 25th Division and in our 2/34th Tank Battalion that the units of the division were being shut down so that the division, nominally, could be returned to its official base in Hawaii. For this reason we abandoned Tay Ninh and returned to Cu Chi for the process of standing down, which in the case of the medical part of the battalion involved the discarding of much material. In my letter of October 28, I describe an indicative and troubling scene: "Today, for instance, I & my company medics cleaned out our aid bags & burned or otherwise destroyed bandages & countless bottles of pills—It seemed to me an incredible waste; we must have destroyed hundreds of dollars' worth of drugs, but no one would take (in the Army) the opened or even unopened pills, so we had to do it. Rather like the food that mess halls (in the US) throw out or give to pigs rather than to people." My words here once again downplay my true feelings at the time: I was deeply disgusted and angry at this case of absurd waste. But this chore of discarding and destroying was, on so many levels, symbolic of the larger picture: with the US Army in Vietnam, the underlying theme was waste and futility.

In this same letter, however, there was yet another reference to the developing of my profound friendship with Jim Kearney. It now strikes me that I was strangely negligent or casual about it at the time, even from when we first met in the summer of 1969 at Fort Sam

Houston in basic training. We had already truly bonded back then, but at the same time, I was not fully aware of the strength or meaning of this relationship. Toward the end of the letter I note that "I have been discussing with my friend, Jim Kearney (in 25th Medical Bn.) the idea of going on a trip through Mexico next summer, and if he can work it out, I think it would be well worthwhile." As it later turned out, we did in fact travel together—in a beat-up VW van—through parts of Mexico, and it was another significant stage of our bonding, as well as an implicit celebration of our return and survival.

What also happened with my transfer from the 25th Division to the 1st Air Cavalry's 15th Medical Battalion was the fortunate reuniting of Jim and me in the same battalion, but also this stretch of my tour was, simultaneously, being put into a safer environment and yet dealing with some of the most traumatic and distressing duties that I faced during my whole tour. As I have already said several times, my own experience was marked by truly amazing good luck, mainly thanks to being in the tank battalion (which was rarely in harm's way) and also to just never being in the wrong place at the wrong time. But at the base-camp clearing station at Phouc Vinh, I not only covered routine sick call duties at the station office but also had the truly dreadful duty to open the body bags of the dead soldiers, find their identifications, and fill out the paper work. In none of my letters home do I make even the vaguest mention of this task. And once again, I knew then and I know even more acutely now why that task and those sights could not ever have been mentioned.

This part of my time in Vietnam would persist in my memory, but largely and for many years below the surface. I remembered, but I also suppressed. The story would return many years later and in strange and startling ways. Only recently, in 2018, a sudden discovery hit me, and I wrote the following:

Dog Tags

I found them unexpectedly when I
went through a chest of drawers the movers

hastily had packed with bedding, towels,
and things that didn't quite belong together.

But fallen to the back and totally unchanged,
my dog tags from nearly fifty years ago,
still on the key-chain I'd worn around
my neck, always there against my chest

for nineteen months, almost a part of me,
in uniform or shirtless in Vietnam heat.
So unremarkable, yet they'd been kept,
as if an accident of negligence or time.

Yet I can't banish from my darkest recalling
those other dog tags I'd try to find when I
had to open the body bags and identify
the soldier, and I'd think: "his name, his name."

However, in a passage of the long letter of December 8 I did break a
bit with my custom of evasion and I describe—though without excessive detail—one episode of incoming casualties. As I wrote it up:

> Very early this morning, a little before 5 am, while I was on the
> desk we got a call from the Medevac people saying that they
> had 11 litter casualties coming to our emergency room & in
> about ½ hour the helicopters began bringing them in, 3 or 4 at
> a time. They were Vietnamese from a small outpost near Dong
> Xoai which had been mortared and then "over-run" by the VC.
> Among the injured there was one woman & 2 younger boys;
> some of them had some rather bad burns & numerous (but small)
> fragment wounds. We patched them up (all the doctors were
> up & working on them) & gave them IV fluids & sent them to
> Vietnamese hospitals on the helicopters. One man died despite
> all attempts to get him going again.

And as I note a few lines later, "This was the first time I'd ever been
involved in a mass casualty situation." This was true. As I reread this
part, I'm a bit struck by how it is both honest and yet coldly evasive.
My readers back home must have long been imagining that I was

always seeing such scenes of casualties, injuries, and deaths; and now I again wonder if they read this as less than fully honest.

My tour of duty in Vietnam ended with my work at the 15th Medical Battalion's clearing station. There was the Christmas and New Year's Eve of 1970–71, and the last weeks and days in Phouc Vinh. The full month of January 1971 and only about two weeks of February pretty much marked the end of my experience. The very last letter is dated February 2, 1971, and it is very short. It is truly striking to me now how much I filtered the truth and the facts. A telling example is in my penultimate letter, February 1, 1971. In a fairly short and nondescript message I mention that I am at the time in Long Binh, and I state that "I'm visiting a friend who used to be in 2/34th and now works here, as well as seeing another friend who is a patient here." In fact the friend who is "a patient" is much more than that—and I think that I can almost reconstruct my thought or deeper motive for being so vague. The man in question was not merely ill, but rather he was Jim Kearney, my closest friend then and for all the years after. Jim had been shot and wounded on about January 29, 1971, while he was on a medevac helicopter that was trying to rescue some army casualties on the ground. The chopper was damaged and Jim himself was wounded, though luckily not too seriously—shot in the left foot and grazed along his left thigh. The helicopter had to return quickly to the base and Jim jumped off, hopping on his one usable foot, the right. I was there at the clearing station to help him when he arrived.

Much more could be said. But I have to think a little more about the letters and what they were at the time of writing and now what they have become. They create a curious story in which I was deeply enmeshed while at the same time I was trying to stand somewhat detached from the real texture and narrative. This collection of old letters contains, for the most part, a flat and oddly empty series of banalities, the worst kind of mundane chatter. Yet they also conceal a struggle. They represent and perhaps convey the challenge and dilemma of a person trying to be reassuring and sound plausible, while at the same time, consciously or unconsciously, trying to keep the reality concealed. Now they are dead letters, but also the realm of ghosts.

Part II: Letters to a C.O. Friend, What Could Not Be Sent Home

The previous section dealt with the letters that I sent to my parents, some family members, and a few others. Obviously these were self-censored, sanitized letters. But then, very much out of the blue, and from a fitting and perhaps inevitable source, there came a crucial batch of letters, thirty-four in all, that I had forgotten about and that had only recently—and all but accidentally—been rediscovered by a good friend of mine, Jack Hailey, an Amherst College classmate, who had in fact requested and been granted 1-O CO status and who did alternative civilian service, outside of the military. My friend's own related but significantly distinct status was meaningful at the time, and this rediscovery has become even more significant now as I try to reconstruct some of my past. All of this demands a reconsideration and commentary as I continue with this retrieval of the story.

In yet another, more recent rediscovery, Jack found four more letters from me. In these four letters, the picture of the complexity and anguish of that time for both of us—as for so many young men—is brought into even sharper focus. These four letters span a time from September 1968, prior to when I was drafted, to April of 1970, when I was then in Vietnam. They reflect the intensity, the sense of threat, and the moral challenge that the Vietnam War held over us, given the very real possibility of Jack or me being called up. Although unfortunately I have not preserved Jack's original letters to me during this time, the impact and witness—to use a penetrating term—of these short documents are vividly present there.

Most amazingly, on the reverse side of one long letter there is found the nine-page typewritten text of part of my request to my draft board, the case in which I argue for my request for 1-A-O status. Thus, although our dialogue is partly truncated due to the absence of Jack's original letters to me, this whole series of letters shows how, at the outset, this close and influential friend was a crucial connection of conscience and moral support for me. The string of letters also indirectly but convincingly reveals how our relationship during my time in the army, and even before, was also a way for me to reach out and make sense of a frequently incredible reality. Such was this dialogue between two different COs, one in the army (a 1-A-O) and the other back in the civilian world (a 1-O).

During my time in the army, from July of 1969 to February of 1971, I wrote several letters to Jack. There are thirty-eight so far that he has been able to retrieve. In these letters I speak mainly about what I was seeing, thinking, and reading. In fact many of the letters read like informal pieces of literary criticism. This makes sense, given that reading as many books as I could get my hands on while in Vietnam was both a continuation of my life as a graduate student and a coping mechanism. Put simply, I have always loved to read. And so this reading was a way to deal with the boredom and anxiety of my life in the army, not only during the stress and tedium of training while in the States but even more so in Vietnam, given the very different stress, routines, and efforts to survive with my spirits intact.

Another element of these letters is that they are a corrective to the more restrained letters that I sent to my parents. In some of them I describe in rather graphic and honest detail a few of the more gruesome encounters that I had and the tasks that I had to perform. These were events that I could in no way have described or even alluded to in the letters written to my parents and other family members. For this reason, along with the more or less trivial remarks and the detours into literary commentary, my letters to Jack gave me a crucial vehicle or outlet for the necessary defense of my emotional state, allowing me to unburden myself—even though one can never truly unburden oneself—of the experiences of the war and, in particular, of my duties as a medic.

As I mentioned above, Jack had applied for and been given 1-O status. Thus he was a CO in the fullest sense, and under this status he performed alternative service outside of the military. His alternative work was with a preschool in California, and as it turned out, this led to his future career as a specialist in early childhood education. In any case, while my letters did not dwell on our partly related but very different CO statuses, this implicit relationship existed as a subtle background to my thinking and experience. I think that I needed to speak with Jack about what I saw and went through because he also was making a sacrifice, he also was caught up—though in a different way—in the challenge of conscience that the Vietnam War brought upon our society and especially upon the young men who were liable to be called up. At the same time, I knew instinctively that Jack had a deeper sympathy and a particular understanding of the feelings and anguish that, in my narratives, lurked behind the seemingly trivial chat about books and that, in other places, came out in blunt and often graphic force. A few of the grim incidents that I presented were deeply troubling. Were they merely war stories? Or were my notes a sincere attempt to make sense of that time and place?

For so many of the American soldiers in Vietnam, the folly of this particular action was more than obvious. Although we knew that it was futile to judge or complain at any great length to friends back home, one could not avoid a periodic comment. In the letter of January 24, 1970, I note that "being in the thick of it certainly does not help one's perspective or judgment. I think [that] when it's all over, we'll look back with the same sort of un-comprehension that our leaders betray right now. The Episode (of Vietnam) will grow less & less significant in our minds & no doubt in the minds of the Vietnamese; just a brutal, absurd & nightmarish straying from the main shape and progression of human events." In this comment I may have been right about the absurdity, but I was wrong about the episode growing less significant. Rather, it would be remembered, distorted, and reused in a variety of unfortunate ways. But over time its force and influence over the concerns and imagination of later generations, especially the young, now in the twenty-first century, seems to have diminished.

In my letters home to my family, along with protecting them from the most distressing experiences, I tended to keep my more cynical views to myself. My letters to my CO friend, Jack, thus gave me the place to express more markedly negative opinions. In particular, and especially given my role as a medic and my further distance from the norms of the army by being a 1-A-O, I was inclined to see and point out the distortions and hypocrisy of much that went on. In a particularly blunt passage in the letter of March 13, 1970, I note this reality. Perhaps it reflected and resulted from my prior identity as a student of literature. As I said to Jack, about his desire to share my letters with others, "You may edit at will and as needed, you may even distort and invent, if it be appropriate; life is a bit like that and so is Vietnam— it is largely invented, imagined and arbitrarily defined—i.e., people really *do* die and get hurt, but we invent the justification for why it was to happen—and sometimes we must even invent and fictionalize the *What* of what they were doing at the time." Oddly enough, and as fate would have it, a few weeks later I was pulled from the field and ordered back to battalion headquarters to serve as an awards clerk, a job that I was told (and that I thought) would only be temporary, but in fact proved to be an illegal and inappropriate order from the battalion command. As I point out in another passage, in "Letters Home," I soon had to insist on leaving that duty.

Did my identity as a noncombatant, both the nature of my 1-A-O category and the simple fact that I had never been given weapons training, affect how I viewed the basic and routine actions of the men around me, the regular combatants? Clearly it did. People then and even now, much later, sometimes have asked me how I could have been an unarmed soldier in this war zone. And I have tried to explain the limits defined by the 1-A-O status. Once, in Vietnam and with 2/34th Armored, a regular combatant soldier asked me that question and I replied "Well, if you do your job, I'll just do mine." I was fearful, of course, but I was also fatalistic: if my number were to come up (death), then that would be it.

But I did wonder about what the role, training, and obvious duty of the regular soldiers around me meant to their thinking and sensibility. Perhaps I could never really understand their situation or feelings—and I don't really presume to claim that knowledge—but in one letter (March 25, 1970) I speculate on this question. As I put it, "What can a man be? He is little else but, at all times when it is necessary, the outward manifestation of the urge for survival; and 'if I must kill you, I will necessarily learn to *hate* you.' And perhaps I will do this without even needing or ending up in hating myself. We all wish to endure; and malice, antagonistic hatred, is at least one of the many protocols or modes of assuring our persistence." Of course this view of things, this pronouncement, which now strikes me as unduly authoritative, really cannot speak for any others, the men who had to fight and who were often at greater risk than I was. As I say elsewhere, my several assignments were lucky for me: I was usually either farther away or not in the wrong place when random shit hit the fan. However, it was impossible to avoid the sense of fear of being in Vietnam, in that place and at that time.

For all of the men and women who found themselves in Vietnam, there were and are unique and often painful, complex stories. No one individual's reflections can come near to capturing the full truth or the "correct" judgment of that time and place. Each person who was there and was fortunate enough to come home alive has his or her own respective story. I respect all of those who went. To this day I ponder and consider their views. For me the experience was peculiar, partly due to my good luck (where I was stationed and all the extreme violence I luckily escaped) and partly due to my identity not just as a medic but as an unarmed 1-A-O medic.

As I read through the letters to Jack, I find myself recovering much of the painful thought that I went through in the process of taking this decision and making my case. These thoughts and my reasoning come out to a small degree in the two letters from September and October 1968. But in addition, as I now can see much more clearly, my correspondence with my 1-O friend was a crucial lifeline, an anchor, and also a vehicle that helped me keep some sanity.

I was a medic, which obviously meant that my principal job was to take care of others, mostly with their physical and medical needs.

But my role as a medic at times implicitly tasked me with trying to calm and reassure others. Sometimes it had to do with reassurance about an illness, infection, or wound, but other times they needed something more like moral support about being there in the war. I don't know if I did a good enough job in that area. But perhaps my success or failure can only be gauged by the feelings of the other men, those whom I tried to help. Now, so many years later, for the most part, those opinions and memories are largely inaccessible.

The duties laid upon me also included dealing with the disposition of the dead, as I have described in episode two ("The Death of Billy Caldwell") of chapter 4, "Things We Saw on the Ground." This was hard. My letter of April 13, 1970, details this grim experience. Nonetheless, I doubt that what I had to do was more difficult or more horrible than what other men—combatant soldiers and many other medics—encountered.

Like the letters that I wrote to Jack, another of my ways of coping, as I now have come to realize, was the intense, voluminous reading and the writing that I did while in Vietnam. Most of my writing took the form of the many letters that I sent out, while some other writing ended up in a small notebook that became the set of poems, thirty-two at the time, that were later published as *The Vietnam Typescript*. Overall my writing—whether letters or poems—provided a mode of dealing with the time and the place. But I now realize that this writing was also the unintended laying of a debt that decades later I would be required to acknowledge and confront.

In all of this, my writing relationship with Jack was immensely important. As I neared the end of my tour, which ended with my departure from Vietnam on February 17, 1971, I wrote a letter that in part described a too-common horrible scene and that also tried to express my sense of my mission, my own experience, and what much of Vietnam meant to me. This penultimate letter (January 4, 1971) clearly reflects the importance of writing as part of my lifeline. Knowing that Jack was an especially appropriate reader, it was something that I wanted and needed to say to him, as I was anticipating the end of my tour of duty. Part of what I wrote in that letter is the following:

> I keep trying to write: the Vietnam experience hasn't been exhausted by me, but I have been exhausted ... by it. ... I wish to tell you something, but it is too arduous for a letter, I guess. ...
>
> It's nearly over, but in a way there's still much for me to do: I must stay (or try to stay) alert and sensitive up to the very end—to note down (if one can) that tact & texture of the temporal & emotional experience, to cite the wounds on the sensibility as I have to, simultaneously, write cards on the nature of the physical wounds, broken skin, bones, as in a young men—21 years old, 6', 160 lb., a handsome sensitive face—killed this last evening by a head-wound; I didn't know his religion, but the Catholic Chaplain came & said the last rites—somehow only the tired yet humble, utter *routine* of the Catholic terminology can give anything to these desperate, pathetic, post-ultimate moments, the body already quite dead, a grace & handsomeness of mere flesh locked in a dreadful stasis—finally at peace.
>
> Yes, I have much to do. It's 1971 & every prayer that goes up is a plea for peace; but the man of us will not achieve peace; rather Peace—death, violent or otherwise—will overtake & rejoin the man, us. Many times I am a witness, shaken by the un-ugliness & the fearful familiarity of this cold & gentle serenity, the ultimately closed eyes.

And so my fourteen months and ten days of service in Vietnam was drawing to its conclusion, a fortunate one for me. Jack's rediscovery of my letters to him now can clearly be understood as part of the recovery of this complicated past, a past in which I—a kind of pacifist, a CO—found myself in the thick of things, absurdly in harm's way, unarmed but making a presence and a witness to violence, injury, and death. Although I was indeed there, at that time and in that place, I cannot make any claim to having a privileged perspective or any sort of moral superiority. Each soldier who participated and found himself in Vietnam had his own sense of moral value, be it of an honest commitment to the ostensible military objectives, or be it opposition and a negative, critical view.

With the end of the draft in 1973, any integral presence of the 1-A-O CO medic in the army is no longer a possibility. And even more tellingly, it has become almost incomprehensible to far too many Americans. The military authorities are probably pleased that this is so. While I am sincerely glad that, at present, young men and now women are spared the possibility of involuntary conscription into the military, I feel that this new policy is not without its negative consequences and its inevitable influence—or lack of influence—on our society. As Binyamin Appelbaum, in his recent book *The Economists' Hour*, has stated, with the ending of the draft in 1973, "War, once an abnormal act of national purpose, has become a regular line of work."[1] I can't help but wonder if this voluntary state of affairs is necessarily better for our society, culture, and for the men and women who now neither know nor are fully able to comprehend the meaning of this lost identity.

Chapter 8

Medevac Medic

(*Kearney*)

In September 1970 the 25th Infantry Division, where I now made my home, received orders to stand down, the second division to do so as part of the Nixon-Kissinger plan to wind the war down. For me this meant, once again, reassignment within country, my new orders this time bringing me to the 1st Cavalry (Airmobile) stationed at Phuoc Vinh to the northeast of Saigon. Bill Clamurro also received orders for the 1st Cavalry. Upon arriving at headquarters at Phuoc Vinh, I volunteered for medevac straightaway and was accepted. Here a word of explanation is in order.

Though there had been early first steps in this direction during the Korean War, the whole concept of relying on helicopters to evacuate the wounded really took shape during the Vietnam War. In referring to Vietnam, the terms *dust-off* and *medevac* are often used interchangeably, but there was a distinction. The several dust-off units had their own command and control and their own birds, which meant that they operated independently of the various army divisions. Medevac, on the other hand, was integral to the 1st Air Cavalry Division, as part of the whole air mobile concept that the 1st Air Cavalry had pioneered.

Both, however, performed the same function. A further distinction is that the dust-off choppers, in nominal compliance with the Geneva Conventions, were not armed, whereas the medevac choppers of the 1st Air Cavalry were equipped with dual M-60 machine guns.[1]

When I volunteered for medevac I knew it would be dangerous, but, on the other hand, I would have a roof over my head, tolerable food to eat, and every fourth day off—all luxuries in Vietnam. I was also an experienced medic by this point. I had already received three Army Commendation Medals, one with *V* for valor, and had gained that professional confidence that only comes with experience. All medics will know what I mean by this. I also have to confess that there was a prestige factor. I had come to admire (and even envy) the dust-off and medevac crews I had worked with in my previous assignments, and I just wanted to be part of a unit with an ethos dedicated to saving rather than taking lives, as encapsulated in the motto "So that others may live." It was also an assignment wholly consistent with my beliefs as a CO.

Medevac was, by and large, all volunteer. Only seasoned medics and crew members were accepted, while most of the pilots received specialized instruction stateside since this assignment demanded the utmost skill. Only the best would do.

After a brief orientation, I was worked into the rotation and began flying. I flew medevac about four months and logged a total of fifty or sixty missions—a modest number compared to most of my comrades. Despite the danger, which was very real and constant, I loved it. That's all I know to say. The mission was admirable, the camaraderie tight, and the professionalism on the part of both the crew members and the pilots superb. I liked my job so much, as a matter of fact, that it played into my decision to voluntarily extend my tour of duty sixty days. When I mention this to my students, they often shake their heads in disbelief, but for those of us present at the time and place, there is no need for explanation. They understand.

To make matters even better, Bill Clamurro was assigned to the 15th Medical Battalion aid station that was only a short walk from

Medevac headquarters, Phuoc Vinh, winter 1970–71.

"Doc" Kearney in front of a Huey.

Near Tay Ninh, with Nui Ba Dinh faint in background.

Waiting for a mission near Cambodia.

the medevac headquarters and barracks. We spent nearly all our free time together, drinking beer, watching outdoor movies while sitting on benches made of discarded and shot-up helicopter rotors, playing chess in the aid station when he was on duty and I was not, and discussing all sorts of things from politics to Golden Age Spanish literature. Finally I had a friend, someone besides myself to keep company with during the experience of war. It had been a long drought. His presence and our camaraderie helped to make the final months of our tours of duty bearable, even pleasant at times.

Night Desk in Phouc Vinh

The year in Vietnam has nearly come full round
and toward the end one sees that it's not the same
as the year, say, in California,
although it will be measured in similar terms.

As interest fixes on the final days,
the first become unexpectedly clear,
precise as worn familiar photographs.
The middle time, once interminable and vast,
has slipped into a foreign and forgotten past.

A certain balance is demanded of the mind.
To keep a careful list of what it forgets:
the first fearful explosions, the crushed
dead body
of a young blond soldier killed in his sleep,
cool blood still dripping on the gray concrete.

Some images are specifically retained:
a sense of twilight, wordless jungle night;
thoughts on the universal cockroach, more expert
at survival than man or man's bold designs.

And the sounds of distant artillery,
the movement of a rugged dirt road

or the partly shrouded cone of a mountain,
dark and alone on the empty plain,

will become strange, returning powers
fixed in the memory, confounding thought
or understanding, but persistent as the dust.
In this and all my sleeplessness
the time has run. It seems to end, and I am tired.[2]

Occasionally, travelling shows came through for the amusement and/or edification of the troops in the large base camps. The most famous of these was the Bob Hope traveling show, a large production that included a rock band, scantily clad girls dancing suggestively, and, of course, Bob Hope himself. While at Lai Khe I actually had the experience of attending one of his shows. If memory serves me correctly, the event occurred my first week at Lai Khe, before I went out in the field. Bob Hope had done the same thing during World War II and Korea. He was roundly lauded for his efforts in uplifting morale and strengthening resolve. But in Vietnam something was missing. It was no longer the "Good War" of the "Greatest Generation" as popularized by Stephen Ambrose in his book *Band of Brothers*. The troops were enthusiastic enough, but the difference was that here many of them were also discontented and alienated in ways that Bob Hope and his generation found difficult—indeed, impossible—to comprehend. Much of Hope's humor, which attempted to belittle and deride hippies and peaceniks back in the States, fell flat, at least with me. I came away feeling like the whole extravaganza was more propaganda than entertainment. But that was me.

The other large, base-wide event I attempted to attend while in Vietnam was a nondenominational Christmas service. This happened at Phuoc Vinh. At this stage of my life I was an avowed atheist. For his part, Bill had not completely abandoned the church. The music, traditions, and celebrations of the church continued to have deep meaning for him even as he grew skeptical about many of the church's core beliefs. We often had discussions along these lines, and he attempted

Bob Hope with Eva Reuber Staier (Miss World 1969) in Vietnam.
From William Geist, ed., *The First Infantry Division in Vietnam, Vol. 3: 1969*
(San Francisco: US Department of the Army, 1970).

to soften my stance, which he felt was unduly harsh and dogmatic in its own right. In line with this, he invited me to attend the Christmas Eve ceremony hosted by the base chaplain. I was not on duty that night and reluctantly agreed to go along.

To our surprise, when we reached the large tent where the service was to be held, the chaplain stood outside the tent, not for the purpose of greeting and welcoming the soldiers to the service but rather to ensure that those attending were properly groomed and attired according to army regulation. When it came our turn, neither Bill nor I passed inspection and were turned away since neither had our rank insignia on the lapels of our blouses. I had never encountered such nit-picking in regard to uniform regulations before in Vietnam, and it struck me as odd that of all persons it should come from a chaplain. His rigidity seemed, sadly, contrary to the Christmas spirit that he was there to celebrate. I am afraid this little episode did little to soften my stance against organized religion, but it was, in its own way, revealing.

Our area of operation (AO) was a flat expanse of triple canopy jungle that stretched practically unbroken in a broad arch from the northeastern fringes of Saigon all the way to the Cambodian/Laotian border, its vastness interrupted only by that odd and iconic geologic feature known as Nui Ba Dinh, the Black Virgin Mountain. In contrast with the previous areas in and around Lai Khe and Cu Chi, there was very little VC activity here. It was solid NVA territory. With the thick jungle for cover, the NVA had set up numerous infiltration routes from their sanctuaries across the border into the Saigon area. The 1st Cavalry's mission was to interdict these routes, with the result that after the Tet Offensive of 1968, which had featured several large set battles involving hundreds of troops on both sides, our AO had settled into a cat-and-mouse ambush war with frequent, intense, but usually brief firefights at the squad or platoon level.

The crews at Phuoc Vinh Medevac flew a rotating schedule of first-up, second-up, third-up, and then a full day off. Having every fourth day off was quite a luxury in Vietnam, as most did not have any time off at all, laboring even on Sundays and holidays. It was a tacit recognition of the very real danger we faced when flying, but I suspect it was also as much for the helicopters as for the crews. Helicopters are very complicated machines, and even the most sturdy and reliable among them—and certainly the Hueys we flew counted as such—require continual maintenance, much more so than your average fixed-wing aircraft. The fourth day of rest allowed the crew chiefs to thoroughly inspect their machines and to do routine maintenance.

The first-up crew was on twenty-four-hour standby for any mission that involved combat casualties. The crew, dressed and ready to launch at a moment's notice, remained in the headquarters control room, which was located in an old French colonial house across from the helipad where the machines were parked in sand-bagged revetments. In quiet periods the crew would sometimes watch 8 mm movies, or play cards or dominoes, or just sit around with every man doing his own thing, like catching a little shut-eye, listening to music, or writing letters. Second-up was likewise on twenty-four-hour standby, but the crew members were not required to stay in the headquarters, if memory serves me correctly. In any case, the role of second-up was, as the name suggests, to fly backup to first-up, should first-up encounter problems or if there were multiple casualty situations. Third-up generally backhauled patients who had either suffered serious wounds or succumbed to some other serious disease or malady that required more serious medical care than the field aid stations could provide. These patients were flown, as a rule, to the 24th Evacuation Hospital near Saigon.

Of the three rotations, third-up actually supplied some of the more unusual, memorable, and, on a couple of occasions, scary situations. In addition to American casualties, we also backhauled ARVN soldiers, Montagnard mercenaries, and occasionally Vietnamese civilians. The ARVNs, rightfully or wrongfully, were not held in high esteem by most American servicemen. The general view was that they were unreliable allies who could not be trusted when the chips were down. We were often called on to pick them up from the field for what seemed to us minor ailments, such as rashes or fevers. To use the army lingo of the time, they were shammers, or goldbrickers, which we resented mightily since all pickups from the field, even cold pick-ups, could easily turn hot and deadly at the drop of a hat. Harboring this resentment and prejudice, we often took this as an invitation to hone our skills, whether needed or not, especially the skill of start-ing an IV of saline solution. Many an ARVN with a minor scratch departed the chopper carrying an IV bag attached to his arm or the

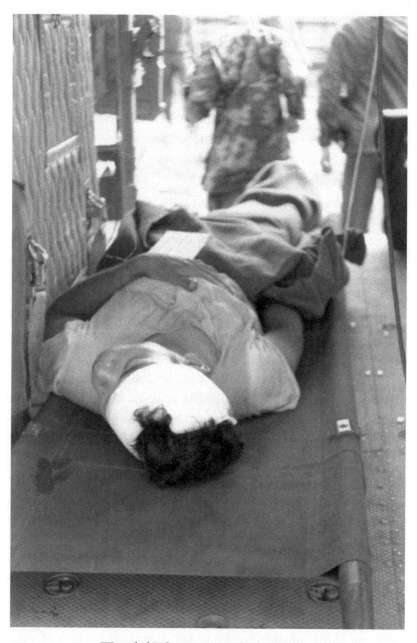

Wounded VC receiving medical attention.

back of his hand. But occasionally we picked up people with exotic injuries attendant to living in the jungle, such as snake bite, tiger mauling, or lightning strike. One of my fellow medics even delivered a baby on board the chopper.

Two of these backhaul missions came close to being my demise. In the first one, we had flown to a forward base camp located somewhere along the Cambodian-Laotian border in order to pick up several GIs with various wounds and afflictions requiring hospitalization. It appeared to be a routine mission. None of the patients were ambulatory, so it was necessary to suspend them from litters crossways in the bay of the helicopter. This made it possible to have four litters, one above the other, and still have some room in the bay of the chopper for the medic to move around and work and to take on one or two more ambulatory patients, if necessary. The patient in the top litter, we were informed, had overdosed on heroin or some other drug. He seemed passive and inert, so the medics on the ground had not strapped him to his litter—a big mistake. We had no sooner reached cruising height— around four thousand feet—when I noticed the druggy had revived.

He lifted his head and noticed a strap dangling from the ceiling of the chopper, which terrified him. With a start, he yelled, "Snake!" and sprang from his litter and attacked me, attempting to fling me from the helicopter—the side doors being wide open, as usual—and I was in no way tethered to the machine. With one hand I took an iron grip to the pilot's seat and with the other I attempted to fight him off, but he was a very strong dude, completely out of his gourd. Luckily the gunner— Kramer, I believe it was—came to my rescue. A very powerful person himself, he coldcocked the drug-crazed patient with one blow, knocking him completely senseless. We quickly put him on a spare litter, and using medic's tape we straightjacketed him to the litter so that when we arrived, he looked like a mummy, completely unable to wiggle.

I am occasionally asked if I experience recurrent nightmares about Vietnam. "Yes," I reply, "I do." One of the most common and frightening is the fear and dread of falling to my death. Unfortunately, as I grow older, it is a nightmare that is becoming increasingly frequent.

Another adventure involved an all-instrument nighttime mission during the monsoon season to a forward FSB along the Cambodian border, perhaps FSB Buttons, in the vicinity of Song Be. Our mission was to backhaul a patient who had life-threatening wounds. To fly a 100 percent instrument mission in the dark of night in the middle of a monsoon storm is a feat that very few pilots would attempt, but it is one that medevac pilots routinely undertook in line with our motto "So that others may live"—a real testament to their incredible skill as pilots and dedication as medevac crew members.

But even for the very best, such a mission was always, by definition, inherently dangerous, and on his particular mission, we all came very close to dying. We lifted off and struck a compass course for the base. It was pitch black and raining cats and dogs. We flew like this in silence a good way, the cabin lit by the eerie orange glow of the large navigation display on the instrument panel, a kind of ball that indicates pitch as well as bearing. This part of Vietnam north of Tay Ninh becomes hilly, even mountainous, and so it was necessary to maintain a certain altitude. The rain was so hard and the night so dark, however, that it was not possible to pick out the lights of the FSB as we approached the general vicinity, or any lights on the ground anywhere, for that matter. For the pilots it was pure compass and dead reckoning.

Finally the commanding officer said over the intercom, "We must be over the base. The radio man below says he thinks he can hear the faint sound of our chopper. Hit the lights." Hueys were outfitted with a very powerful floodlight mounted to the bottom of the helicopter so as to illuminate the ground during nighttime landings and pickups. When the Peter Pilot (copilot) flipped the switch to the floodlight, all we could see were solid sheets of rain coming at an oblique angle to the helicopter. Instantly, everyone in the helicopter got vertigo, that deadly condition of utter disorientation, completely unable to tell up from down. I remember looking at the big orange ball indicating orientation in relation to the ground and not being able to make heads or tails of it.

The commander, completely disoriented, screamed to his Peter Pilot, as the aircraft began a fatal, sliding descent, "Take over, take over!" Unfortunately, he also had succumbed to vertigo, and for a dreadful and terrifying few seconds that seemed an eternity we were headed for either a fatal stall or a crash and death. Luckily, the Peter Pilot snapped out of it in the nick of time and was able to right the aircraft and save our lives. The commander aborted the mission and we made it back to our base. That was certainly one for the books. In July 1971, Brig. Gen. George W. Casey Sr., then commanding general of the 1st Air Cavalry, perished along with his crew when his chopper crashed into the side of a mountain somewhere in the highlands during a nighttime mission in a rainstorm. It was a powerful reminder of how dangerous these missions could be.

Another episode on a third-up mission illustrates some of the weird interpersonal dynamics of the war and the precarious position medics often found themselves in. We had flown to another, larger base for some minor repair to the helicopter that was not possible to get done at Phuoc Vinh. For the crew this meant time to kill. I made my way to the local EM club and was enjoying a cold beer when a grunt fresh from the field and still in his dirty, faded jungle fatigues, which clearly marked him as a grunt, bellied up to the bar next to me. He took one look at me and concluded that I was a medic.

Many medics had the habit of sticking a pair of bandage scissors either in the breast pocket of the regular uniforms or in a pocket on the sleeve of flight uniforms, which I had on. He then addressed me: "You're a fucking medic, aren't you?"

Somewhat taken aback, but a little annoyed, I replied, "Yeah, what's it to you?"

With a quick motion he reached down and pulled a Bowie knife out of his boot, grabbed me by the collar, stuck the knife under my chin, and said, "You fucking medics killed my buddy!"

Looking into his eyes, I could see the grunt had that classic thousand-mile stare typical of soldiers from all wars who had seen and experienced too much, and now were in that gray area between madness and sanity, with a propensity to slide either way. He had slid the wrong way, and my mere presence had set him off.

I apologized profusely and said any and all that I thought he wanted to hear, but the main thing I said was that we were like him, draftees who had been forced into life-and-death situations against our will and with woefully inadequate training. We did the best we could with what we had, but we were human, and so we made mistakes. Couldn't he see it in himself to forgive us?

My words seemed to resonate, and he withdrew his knife and relaxed his grip. But I didn't waste any time and vacated the club before he changed his mind.

The repairs took longer than scheduled and continued into the evening. We heard some shooting, and on inquiry learned that a grunt recently in from the field had gone totally berserk and had begun shooting up the place with his M16. The MPs had then been called with the usual, unfortunate result. I never learned for sure, but I suspect it was the very same soldier who had confronted me. This episode brought home forcibly for me the tremendous pressure that medics in the field had to live with: not only fear of the enemy but also fear of screwing up, and losing the respect of one's own comrades. It is no wonder that so many medics cracked under the pressure.

As I look back, November and December were, relatively speaking, quiet, but things began to heat up dramatically in January 1971. As we now know, as a follow-up to the Cambodian invasion in May 1970, Nixon and Kissinger had launched clandestine missions into Laos to interdict and disrupt the Ho Chi Minh Trail and the sanctuaries located therein. The increased activity on the part of the NVA that we began to experience firsthand in our AO made sense in this context, but it also reflected the fact that the NVA had by this point largely replaced the devastating losses in manpower suffered during the Tet Offensive, on the one hand, while, on the other, it had sufficiently rebuilt its supply and logistics network that the Cambodian invasion in May and June of 1970 had seriously disrupted.

Picking up casualties on the ground.

The NVA was on the move again. Indeed, after January 1, the heat of conflict began to rise again all across Vietnam, with increased activity in all sectors. In the last two weeks alone that I was in Vietnam—that is, from January 15 to January 29, when I was wounded—I flew four separate hot missions, missions where we came under hostile fire, and did two hot hoists, and that was just one crew (there were four full crews stationed at Phuoc Vinh). In one of these missions, the copilot, had his little finger neatly severed by an AK-47 round that came up through the floor bubble.

Chapter 9

Final Mission

(*Kearney*)

The increased activity by the NVA and the heightened danger for the flight crews was concerning. With DEROS scheduled for February 5, 1971, a scant week away, I was looking forward to returning to civilian life, and at this late stage of the game, the thought of being wounded or killed was even more disturbing. Bill and I had both voluntarily extended and by so doing traded an extra sixty days in-country for a five-month early discharge from the army, with our scheduled DEROS also becoming the new discharge date. It was a foolish bet on my part because the extra sixty days were in a war zone, while the remaining five months of service would have been stateside.

Also, anticipating the end of my brief army career, I wanted to convey some sense of what I had experienced as a medevac medic when I returned to "the world." I had recently purchased a cassette recorder, which could be obtained duty-free from the local PX. I had already taped several missions during the preceding two weeks, most of which were routine. I did this by placing the microphone in a spare helmet, stuffing some gauze in it, and then plugging the helmet into the intercom. The result was an almost perfect mix, as if done by a professional, between background noise and radio chatter. One hears clearly the popping of the rotors, the steady hum of the turbine, and (subsequently) the sound of machine-gun fire, but the microphone also picked up distinctly the radio chatter and the intercom exchanges among the crew members.

This set the stage for my final mission, which is preserved for posterity on tape. On the morning of January 29, 1971, I was not on duty. I had my Nomex (special fire-resistant cloth) flight jacket on but otherwise was out of uniform. It was a nice, sunny day and I was sitting on a mound of sandbags outside my hooch listening to my fellow Texan, Janice Joplin, crooning the blues on a cassette tape I had obtained, when someone came running saying there was an urgent mission for first-up but the medic, Doc Burkhardt, was missing (he had come down with a fever and had gone to the aid station). Both second- and third-up were also out on missions. The first-up crew needed a medic to take Doc Burkhard's place. Naturally, I volunteered to fill in, as any of my fellow medics would have willingly done under the circumstances; that was understood.

I quickly grabbed my medic's bag, helmet, and cassette recorder and sprinted for the helipad. The others were there, the preflight check complete, and the motor beginning its slow wind up to full RPM. The ranking pilot was Capt. David Weeks, but Warrant Officer (WO) Greg Simpson was serving as aircraft commander (AC) on this particular mission. If memory serves me correctly, I had not flown with either of these pilots before. David Kramer was the starboard machine gunner, and Mark "Doc" Holiday served as crew chief and manned the M-60 machine gun on the port side of the aircraft. As we lifted off from the helipad and began our ascent past the old French colonial house that served as our headquarters and control center, Weeks filled us in on the particulars of the mission over the intercom. It was to be a hot hoist, the most dangerous situation for a medevac crew.

The 1st Air Cavalry, along with the 101st Airborne Division, had pioneered the air mobile concept. Everything was done by helicopters, including reconnaissance. The division had smaller choppers for this purpose. They would flit around the jungle tops hoping to spot the enemy before they spotted them and opened fire. Unfortunately, this mission began with precisely this scenario. The little Loach recon chopper (a light observation recon helicopter, usually the Hughes OH-6A "Cayuse") had taken fire and gone down. The Blues, a special team for securing downed choppers, had gone in but the NVA had set up an ambush. One of the troopers had received a sucking chest wound, a very serious injury requiring immediate evacuation and a whole-blood transfusion. Although we routinely started transfusions in-flight of saline solution to stabilize blood pressure and prevent or lessen shock, we did not normally do whole-blood transfusions on board, but because of the urgency and severity of the wound, we made an exception on this mission. There was some disagreement about this between me and the AC, which can be heard on the tape, but I was overruled. This required a quick put-down at the aid station to get a bag of blood ,and then off we went. I had objected to getting blood because the medic on the ground had not relayed the wounded man's blood type, so when the AC insisted on blood anyway, I requested universal donor type O negative blood and gambled there would be no reaction, which could be fatal.

This all had taken place, unbelievably, only three or four klicks (kilometers) outside the wire of Phuoc Vinh, the large base camp located forty or fifty miles to the northeast of Saigon that served as headquarters of the 1st Air Cavalry. We were over the area of the action in a matter of two or three minutes. We had difficulty, however, in locating the smoke bomb that had been popped by the troops on the ground to mark the location where we should attempt to descend. This was not surprising, given the density of the jungle. Those who have never really experienced true jungle often have little concept of how impenetrable it can be. The typical woodlands characteristic of South Central Texas where I grew up—dense stands of live oak, pecan, ash, and elm—would barely reach the second level of the fourteen thousand square miles of triple canopy jungle that made up

Dust-off chopper equipped with swing-out hoist, Kearney inside.

the 1st Air Cavalry's AO at this time. So in order to spot the smoke, in this case the color "goofy grape," we had to crisscross the general area until we were directly over the spot when it briefly became visible as a small cloud of purple fog suspended in the dense vegetation below. It took us considerably longer, in fact, to locate the smoke than it did to reach the general area, and our agitated, almost frantic search for the smoke can be clearly sensed from the intercom chatter at this stage of the mission.

Once we did locate it, however, we quickly began our descent in a tight downward spiral from about 1,500 feet toward the target. The crew chief could keep the smoke under observation and talk the pilot down from his vantage point from the side of the helicopter. We routinely flew with the large, barnlike sliding doors open, which afforded great visibility to the crew chief and door gunner. Once we got to the top canopy of the jungle, we could only stovepipe down through a small opening between the trees, with literally inches to spare on either side of the bird. This is where the amazing and necessary partnership between the doormen and the pilots took over. The pilots might as well have been blindfolded, because with only limited visibility, they concentrated instead on the instruments, while being talked down every foot of the way by the crew members. "You're clipping limbs to the left, Dave; two feet to the right. Okay, you're looking good now, bring her on down; about a hundred feet from the ground. You're over the hole now; hold it right there."

The Huey, of course, could not land and instead stopped to hover about fifty feet off the ground. The wash of the blades parted the final layer of bushes and shrubbery to reveal the troopers directly below us hunkered behind whatever cover they could find. One large tree trunk lay laterally across the space, and this is where the medic with a couple of other troopers had placed the wounded man, whom I could clearly see when I edged out the side of the Huey with one foot on the skid in order to get a clear view. I then threw down the special litter outfitted with a D ring for the hoist and sufficient straps to fasten securely an unconscious or severely wounded soldier into the litter, which then could be hoisted vertically rather than horizontally into the helicopter and thus pass more easily through any intervening shrubbery.

The medic on the ground went to work securing his wounded buddy into the litter while I took control of the hoist. I swung the boom of the hoist outside the door and, taking the handheld control in my right hand with one button for up and one for down, I once again stood on the skid for a better view and began lowering the cable. We had been issued so-called chicken plate flak jackets and everyone (luckily) had theirs on except me, which was not unusual for medics. The reason for this was that the inch-thick plates—one for the breast and one for the back, each contained in a kind of net jacket—were bulky and rendered one top-heavy, so much so that the jackets came equipped with a tether and snap so that as you moved around inside the cabin, you couldn't accidentally fall out of the aircraft. Along with most other flight medics, I often chose not to wear the chicken plates, especially during hoists. So, simply put, we often chose to forego this added protection.

With the cable about halfway to the ground, the firefight on the ground erupted anew to break the brief lull during which we had been able to successfully descend. We were afforded a terrifying ringside view, as it were, hovering above the whole spectacle and able to clearly see both the troopers behind their logs and the cleverly concealed NVA bunker as they exchanged automatic weapons fire at practically point-blank range, barely fifty feet apart on the jungle floor below. Spotting the bunker, Kramer, our starboard gunner, also opened up with his M-60, at which point the NVA turned their machine gun on us.

It was like a three-way Wild West shootout but with machine guns instead of six-shooters. This first burst missed me, although I could clearly see the rounds—not as individual bullets, of course, but as the straight lines of the tracers emanating from the bunker and whizzing by on either side of me. Kramer was not so lucky. Veteran machine gunners often fastened C ration cans to the clip on the side of their M-60s, over which the belted 30-caliber machine-gun shells fed more smoothly into the mechanism of the gun. The standard clips issued for that purpose often jammed. In any case, an enemy round hit Kramer's bean can square on, with the result that it exploded, covering my face mask with beans and peppering me with fragments of the can. Another round hit Kramer square in the middle of his chicken plate, which stopped the projectile cold and saved his life, but the massive impact knocked the breath out of him and rendered him momentarily senseless. Still another round clipped the top of his shoulder and embedded in the firewall of chopper behind him.

In the heat and confusion of the moment, I didn't know exactly what had happened. The beans on my face mask—which, for all I knew, could have been Kramer's brains or the blood from the blood bag—obscured my view. It was at this point on the tape that you can hear Doc Holiday yelling, "Kearney's been hit!" to which I reply, "No, I'm not hit but something hit me, the blood or something, goddamn it."

I was kneeling at the edge of the door this whole time, guiding the cable to the ground. But then the NVA ensconced in the bunker below fired a second burst of machine-gun fire, and I was not so fortunate this time. One round came up through the floor of the chopper, thankfully expending much of its energy as it did. It then entered the top of my right foot, the kneeling foot, shattering a bone as it passed completely through the foot only to embed in the sole of my boot. (I still have the bullet as a memento, a 7.62 Kalashnikov armor-piercing, blunt-headed projectile). Another round opened up, almost surgically, the muscle the length of my right thigh but hit no bone. A third round made a clean flesh wound in my right arm just above the elbow but once again missed the bone.

With rounds crashing into the chopper from one end to the other, WO Greg Simpson, who throughout had remained cool and fully in charge, aborted the mission. It was a good thing he did. With multiple oil leaks, fuel pouring out of holes in the floor, and the instruments going crazy, we were a gnat's whisker away from crashing in a fiery inferno on top of the very troopers we were attempting to rescue.

Upon being hit I had instinctively thrown myself back into the chopper, a natural defensive reflex. But I also had the presence of mind to "blow the line" by activating an emergency button mounted on the hoist, as I had been trained to do. Luckily, when we came under fire, the patient was not yet attached to the cable, dangling helplessly somewhere between the chopper and the ground, in which case we would have had to drop him as well. This was a nightmare scenario that many crews had to live with: blowing the line and dropping a patient to certain death but knowing that there was no alternative since not doing so could cause the death of the whole crew as well as the patient.

We were able to climb straight out of the hole and gain enough altitude to possibly autorotate down should the chopper suddenly lose

Door gunner David Kramer (*left*) and Chief Warrant Officer Greg Simpson (*right*) pointing to the bullet hole in the floor. This is the bullet that went through my foot. Courtesy of Greg Simpson.

power. We struck a beeline for the aid station helipad at the base, which, as mentioned, was a scant three or four kilometers distant and clearly visible once we gained altitude. It was a race against time because oil was running out of the transmission, causing it to dangerously over-heat, which would lead at some point to catastrophic failure. But the pilots monitored the gauges as best they could and made the decision to try to make base camp and safety before setting down.

The conversation over the intercom at this point is fascinating, with a clear contrast in attitude between me and the rest of the crew. Oblivious at this point to the very real danger that the helicopter might freeze up and fall out of the sky like a rock, I sound on the tape flippant, almost euphoric, even making light of my own wounds. The reason, of course, is that I was overcome by a sense of relief: I had stared death in the face and managed to escape more or less intact. True, I had been seriously wounded, but as an experienced medic I knew my wounds were not life-threatening. They were confined to my extremities and no arteries had been clipped, so there was no serious bleeding. The adrenalin was still flowing, so I felt no pain whatsoever. The pilots and crew chief, on the other hand, were extremely anxious about the deteriorating state of the chopper; indeed, one senses on the tape a desperate concern: Will we make it?

Luckily the durable Huey held together long enough to safely set down at the aid station helipad. The rest of the crew, including, amazingly, the bruised and slightly wounded door gunner Kramer, quickly detached the hoist assembly from our chopper and sprinted the two hundred yards or so to the revetments where the medevac choppers parked. They commandeered another bird and went straight back to the area and this time—sans medic—successfully hoisted the wounded trooper from the ground. Fortunately the NVA had disengaged by this point and slipped away into the jungle, so they encountered no more hostile fire this time.

It has to be acknowledged that in this particular series of events, the NVA came out ahead. Practicing the strategy of "engaging

Rescued pilots. 1st Air Cavalry Annual, 1970.

the Americans by their belt loops,"[1] they had destroyed two helicopters, wounded several American soldiers, and then vanished into the jungle.

The wounded trooper with the sucking chest wound survived, and a year or so later I received a letter of gratitude from him, which unfortunately I have lost. The crew's action in unhesitatingly going back in and knowingly risking their lives once again underscores and confirms that our motto, "So that others may live," was not a collection of empty words. On the contrary, it captured the ethos that we all adhered to when the chips were down. For this action we all received the Distinguished Flying Cross for heroism, presidential citation.

Doc William "Groucho" Clamurro at Phuoc Vinh.

But aside from the fact that I lost my bet and ended my Vietnam service on such a harrowing note, my final mission was memorable for another reason. As I listen to the tape, I can clearly make out the voice of Groucho, who, as luck would have it, was the medic on duty at the aid station when we landed. His presence closed the circle to our shared military careers, one that had begun at Fort Sam Houston in the summer of 1969 where we had trained to be CO medics and that now ended with Bill rendering first aid to me as a concluding act to our shared army experience even as it ushered in a new chapter. One gesture on Bill's part, however, stands out. True to his Groucho persona, Bill is heard to say on the tape, "Kearney, stop hopping around like a chicken with one leg cut off. Are you shamming again?" He then handed me a cold beer. That, if nothing else, sealed a lifelong friendship.

End of the Tour for J. C. K.
(Originally titled "Leaving the War Zone")

The buildings and these fearful yards
are slowly closing down;
and even in the balance of lost and dead
the gradual skin begins to heal.
Even as so much blood
has pooled on the forests and floors
in its own persistent stench,
our part of time incessantly retreats.
The metal was a sudden message,
tearing bone and flesh to wake
us from our evasive hope
and linking once again with you
the fact and possibilities of time.
So you shall live,
the wound was slight,
and many in fact will have lived.
But your blood, diminished pain, relief,
and the tremors of your second thoughts
will only prove that we have not escaped.

The black birds swirl again
about a shallow pond,
and the aircraft continue to land
with the torn and bloodied men,
and at some point it ends.
The bullet also tore a consciousness.
Our questions came full round,
told the fragility and the loss
of an adventure drawing us
with it to the end.[2]

Chapter 10

Nostos (Homecoming)
(*Kearney*)

My homecoming began when I was wounded and ended with my discharge from the army five months later. My wounding had canceled any thought of an early discharge. I was evacuated that same day by helicopter from Phuoc Vinh to the 24th Evacuation Hospital in Saigon. This was an adventure in itself because while waiting in the medevac chopper designated for the backhaul—this time as patient rather than medic—the sirens went off, signaling either a mortar or rocket attack, and rather than unload and seek safety, we just sat there in the helicopter until we got the all clear. It was a freaky situation.

It was night now, my wounds were beginning to throb, and there we sat, unsure of exactly what was happening but clearly hearing the sirens wailing and the incoming detonating over the noise of the idling helicopter. A gentle rain had begun to fall, and the dampness refracted and amplified surreally the effects of numerous illumination flares that filled the sky. I felt very helpless and vulnerable. But soon enough we got the all clear for takeoff and off we went for the twenty minute or so flight to Saigon. Once we arrived at the 24th, my wounds were thoroughly dressed and I was administered morphine to alleviate the pain. After the excitement of the mission had subsided and the adrenaline had worn off, the pain of the shattered bones in my foot intensified, hence the morphine.

The effect of the morphine was extraordinary. I had never had a drug so powerful. I can still remember the pain simply lifting after the injection, as with a curtain rising. I then began to hallucinate. I was looking intensely at the enormous, centuries-old, moss-laden, live oak that covered the backyard of the ranch house where I grew up in Texas and the tree in which I had spent many happy hours climbing as a child. The image was so vivid and clear that I could see and touch and smell the texture of the bark in minute detail. Why that image should come to mind and why it was so powerful that I can still recall it vividly to this day remains a mystery to me. But soon thereafter I drifted off into a deep sleep.

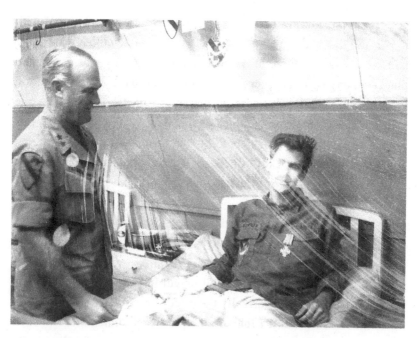

Receiving Distinguished Flying Cross from commanding
general of 1st Air Cavalry.

It was after one of these morphine-induced slumbers that I was rudely awakened to find the commanding general of the 1st Air Cavalry, Brig. Gen. George W. Putnam, along with several aides, standing before me. I was quite groggy and never fully came to my senses. But the aides propped me up while the general pinned the Distinguished Flying Cross for heroism on my chest. The aid then took a Polaroid snapshot, which was given to me, and the party quickly disappeared. I treasure the photo, even though it is smeared, but I have no memory of the actual event.

After a week or so at the 24th Evacuation Hospital, I was flown in a giant cargo jet, outfitted to accommodate the wounded along with the rest of its cargo, to Camp Jama, Japan. I stayed in a large ward of the hospital outfitted with curtains to offer some modicum of privacy for the patients. My chief memory of this place was of one particular sergeant who snored so loudly that it kept the whole ward awake. How a human being could generate so much noise and still remain asleep himself was beyond me. He entertained the whole ward. Another memory was of watching a John Wayne war movie, *Sands of Iwo Jima*, I believe it was, with John Wayne dubbed to speak Japanese. The irony inherent in that still gives me a chuckle after all these years.

After a couple of weeks at Camp Jama I was again placed on an enormous C-141 cargo jet, this time on a stretcher suspended from the ceiling with straps, for my trip back to "the world." In addition to the twenty or so stretcher patients dangling from the ceiling, there were seats for a score or so of ambulatory patients. The trip back was, to say the least, a very different experience than the ride over on a commercial jet complete with smiling, bubbly stewardesses, as if we were all on a vacation excursion to an exotic land. The physical space inside the belly of the plane was cavernous, and once the plane lifted off the ground, the wheels actually retracted into the belly with much creaking and groaning. One could actually see and hear the cables that controlled the rear flaps of the wings as they did their business. We flew nonstop from Japan to Travis Air Force Base near San Francisco, where we were to refuel, change crews, and then continue to Fort Sam Houston, our final destination.

When we took off, however, a red light flashed, and the pilot was forced to abort the takeoff at the very last moment. The plane braked so violently it caused the litters suspended from the ceiling to sway wildly—a frightening and unpleasant sensation, which was exacerbated by the horrifically loud screeching of the braking tires. Due to the mechanical problem, we were forced to deplane and spend the night at the base. I ended up in a pleasant, semiprivate room equipped with a TV with one other patient, a Black man with a wonderful sense of humor. We were laughing ourselves silly watching the "Three Stooges" on our TV and basking in the thought that we were finally safe and sound back in the world, when a sudden and violent shaking rudely interrupted our reveries. An earthquake had struck, and a rather strong one at that—my first experience of such a thing. All I could think was, "Holy cow, will I ever make it back in one piece to Texas and home?"

The following day we resumed our flight back to Fort Sam Houston, where I ended my army career at the very base where it had begun. Once there I was transferred to an orthopedic ward housed in a very old, multistory building from the nineteenth century that went by the improbable name Beach Pavilion. It was not a pavilion and the nearest beach was more than one hundred miles away, so how it had come to be called by this wildly inappropriate name mystified me, and I never got a satisfactory explanation. At all events, the building had obviously been repurposed to be a hospital ward for orthopedic injuries, and it was so overcrowded that I was assigned a bunk in the hallway of the main foyer, which was entertaining, since I could keep an eye on all the goings and comings.

Here I languished for several months, awaiting my turn at the operating table. During the wait I received several visits from various friends and acquaintances, which were very much appreciated but always awkward. Neither I nor they, it seemed, knew what to say. My parents also paid one visit during this time. It was also uncomfortable, but it had the effect of breaking the ice and moving us closer toward reconciliation.

After my turn for surgery finally rolled around, they outfitted me with a cast so that I could now walk with the help of crutches. They always said the long wait was to ensure that no infection was sewn into the wound, but I think that was only partially true. The true reason was that they were grossly understaffed and there was a very long cue for the single orthopedic surgeon, whose name, oddly enough, I can still remember: Dr. Abudah.

Now that I had a cast on my leg and my foot, I became eligible for a pass to go home for several days. In order to obtain the pass, I had to personally apply to the first sergeant whose office was in a different building a couple of blocks removed from Beach Pavilion. I made my way on crutches with difficulty because it was still painful to put any weight on my foot, even though it was in a cast. The sergeant behind the desk—from his appearance a bona fide lifer—took one look at me and told me perfunctorily that he would not grant my request until I got a haircut. I went berserk, the one time in my army career I did so.

I had done my duty. I had lived up to my side of the bargain as a 1-A-O medic. I had come close to death on several occasions and had been severely wounded. I had been awarded medals for both heroism and competence. I had not had a single day's leave since R&R to Hong Kong nearly a year before. I had idled away time in various hospitals for months, awaiting surgery, and now I was denied a pass to go home because my hair was too long. How was I supposed to get a haircut in any case? I saw red and went after the lifer with my crutch. He screamed and kept his desk between us until the executive officer in the office behind him rushed to his rescue and intervened, fortunately, before I was able to whack him. The sergeant was furious, but the officer, quite remarkably, took my side and granted my request for leave on the spot. He also told me that I was due to be formally presented several other belated decorations—the Bronze Star with V, Air Medal with V, and the Purple Heart—in an awards ceremony scheduled for the following week. I thanked the officer but, now thoroughly disgusted with the army and chafing to be a civilian once again, I notified him that I would rather not participate in the awards ceremony, which was in any case a formality. The awards were mine, and they are very meaningful to me. I display them on a plaque on my wall to this day, and the thought of renouncing them as a gesture of defiance, as John Kerry did, never seriously occurred to me.

To get home I took a taxi to downtown San Antonio, where I hopped a Greyhound bus for Houston. When we got in the vicinity of the ranch between Weimar and Columbus, I pulled the cord and the driver stopped and let me out beside the road. With a small bag and on crutches, I laboriously made my way across a neighbor's pasture and past their house for a half mile or so to the Home Place house, nestled in the shade of the giant, patriarchal live oak that I had so vividly visualized while under the influence of morphine— the only house I had ever lived in, a place and a space so far removed from everything I had experienced. The timeless charm and tranquility of the old homestead was totally removed from the troubled world outside its purview. It was good to be home—a real *nostos*.

My parents gave me space, and I just enjoyed being removed from the army and its ways after so many months. I also enjoyed the food. Finally, some real Texas BBQ. One of the things that struck me forcibly was that once again one could venture into the country-side and not be afraid of booby traps or ambush. Here nature was welcoming and not menacing. But once lost, innocence in even such simple matters is difficult to regain.

After the week's leave, I drove my own car, which had been parked at the ranch, back to the base, but my scheduled date for discharge from active service, the so-called ETS (enlisted termina-tion from service date), was fast approaching, which created some-thing of a dilemma. I was far from fully recovered, with a cast still on my leg and foot, bandages on my thigh and arm, and wounds that were still suppurating. The only way I could get around was on crutches or in a wheelchair. I was informed that in order to continue with my convalescence at Fort Sam Houston, or even to apply for the 20 percent disability to which I was entitled, I had to voluntarily extend my active duty status for another six months. There was no way on God's green earth that was going to happen, so I and the US Army parted ways on July 8, 1971, two years to the day from my induction. As far as I was concerned, they could keep their disability and I would tend to my own wounds from this point on. I had lived up to my side of the 1-A-O bargain, but the deal had now expired.

Upon discharge I drove straight from San Antonio to Austin, where I hung out for a few days at the German House and reconnected with those old friends and acquaintances who were still in Austin. But things had changed. *Panta rei*, as Heraclitus famously said, and I soon realized that it was impossible to pick up where I had left off. This was a common experience for returning veterans from all wars at all times.

In the meantime, Bill Clamurro and I had remained in contact. Bill had completed his tour of Vietnam only a few days after I was wounded and had already been a free man for several months when I was finally discharged in July. He had spent this time mainly in New Jersey at his parents' house while sorting his life out and applying to resume his doctoral studies at the University of Washington.

Now that I was also free, we decided that we needed to take the trip together to Mexico that we had discussed while in Vietnam. Bill was fluent in Spanish and had spent the summer of 1966 while in college doing charity outreach work. He loved the country and had often spoken fondly of his stays there and the friends he had made. I, on the other hand, had never ventured past the border towns of Nuevo Laredo or Piedras Negras, notorious for their wide-open bars and brothels, and had little concept of the country and culture beyond the border.

For our trip, which lasted over a month in the fall of 1971, I found an old VW transport van that I repurposed to be a self-sufficient camper. Indeed, we camped most of the time either along isolated beaches or in RV parks, or simply parked alongside the road somewhere, cooking our own meals from the food we bought at local markets or sampling the regional fare from various out-of-the-way restaurants and cantinas, and then laying out our bedrolls at night under a large tarp attached to the side of the van.

Along the way we occasionally stayed with friends Bill knew as we slowly made our way from San Francisco, where we had rendez-voused, down the coast of Mexico to Guadalajara and Mazatlán, and from there into the highlands of the central plateau. It was a marvelous time. We visited some of the isolated mountain communities that Bill had come to know on his college visit. One of these communities, Ixtapan del Oro, located in the western part of the state of Mexico, was almost like a Shangri-La: peaceful, charming, and isolated from the outside world. We had many adventures but all of a harmless nature, and never once did we feel endangered or threatened. It was an innocent time, and a fitting conclusion to our Vietnam experience, with ample time to sip margaritas, savor the food, relish the scenery, admire the many rich and ancient traditions of Mexico, and reflect on our shared experiences. Bill wrote a poem to me during the trip that I now cherish:

Later Dialogue
For James Kearney

The wall becomes the varied dialogue
of stone and each mark of its time,
the process of its persistent place.

And mere movement is sensed
In terms of our differences with
the ruling texture of rock.

Perhaps in something of this way
his body, witness of a war,
is also the catalogue of marks.

The nature or secret of his flesh
and bone, the strong but precarious
balance of slender limbs, was

> that a man is but the page
> on which a time of violence
> inscribes its hundred messages.
>
> Gentle now and distant, calm
> like the harmony of stonework
> in the enchantments of a museum,
>
> a tall and gaunt young man thinks
> quietly on the old and haunting stones;
> but now he may speak with them
>
> in clearer terms, for he too knows
> the secret speech of wounds, of marks
> that give a sense to time, the paradox of pain.

Once returned to the States, we both resumed our academic careers, I at the University of Texas and Bill at the University of Washington, but we continued to remain in close touch. Bill made academia his career and rose to become a distinguished and internationally respected scholar of the Golden Age of Spanish literature, with several scholarly books to his credit. Meanwhile, he continued with his music and published several books of poetry on the side. He is now a retired professor emeritus from Emporia State University in Kansas. Unlike me Bill never married, but he has always enjoyed a very wide circle of family and friends, including his own siblings and their families, all of whom he has taken an active and warm interest in.

For my part, I bailed on academia as a career even though I eventually obtained all the degrees necessary to pursue one, including the doctorate. In retrospect it is clear that the university served as a kind of refuge for me until I had digested the experiences of Vietnam sufficiently that I could become functional in society again. I was always (and still am) torn between a love of the cloistered academic life, on the one hand, and the appeal of the outdoor life, on the other. In the end fresh air won out, and after my father stepped down, I returned to manage the ranch where I had grown up.

While a graduate student, I also met a very attractive, intelligent, and motivated young woman whom I had briefly known before going into the army and who had recently graduated with honors from the University of Texas with a degree in art. We became serious, fell in love, and decided to get married. After fifty years we are still together with three grown children and six grandchildren. Bill Clamurro, as might be expected, served as my best man at our small, private wedding and as godfather to my firstborn. Many years later, when my daughter married, Bill performed the service dressed in his doctoral robes in lieu of clerical garb. Only later in life—after thirty-five years as a rancher—did I return to academia as a guest lecturer. It has been deeply gratifying to return to my old alma mater, the University of Texas—for so long and for so many different reasons the other home base in my life—but now as teacher rather than student.

It is a common observation: for those who actually experience the horrors of war firsthand, the war never really ends. Most succeed in suppressing the memories sufficiently to go about their lives. Others are not so fortunate and slip into alcoholism, or drug abuse, or a sad state of general dysfunction for the rest of their lives. Sadly, one of my own classmates from Columbus High School, who had served as an infantry platoon leader in Vietnam, exemplified the latter outcome and finally succumbed to the alcoholism that took over his life. Bill and I were both fortunate in being able to put the war behind us sufficiently to pick up where we had left off and go on with our lives. It was not an easy transition for either of us, but we both succeeded. As our friendship grew and matured, we talked less and less about Vietnam, preferring to concentrate on shared interests and on the day-to-day realities of our lives.

But in the last several years, as the Vietnam War in general fades from memory for the country as a whole, our personal interest revived even as the fiftieth anniversary of our Vietnam service approached. We each began to sense a gnawing insistence, a growing need to come to terms in some meaningful way with the war and our connection to it. It strikes me that this is probably a common reflex that affects most veterans from all wars. But, significantly, Bill and I began this process of reengagement with the past initially as independent endeavors.

Bill had rediscovered, in an old box tucked away and forgotten in the basement of his house in Emporia, a sheaf of papers, a collection of poems he had written in Vietnam in a notebook and later typed up in Seattle. His friends encouraged him to publish them, which he did in 2018 as *The Vietnam Typescript*.[1] His friends and colleagues at Emporia State organized a reading and talk to celebrate the release of the book. It was well-attended, and I was happy to have been a part of it.

For my part, I designed and taught a course at the University of Texas about Vietnam, and I also collaborated with the Bob Bullock Texas State History Museum in Austin on a five-part podcast based on the recordings I had made in Vietnam, including the mission when I was wounded, entitled "Vietnam on Tape."[2] The podcast, referenced at several points in the narrative, was well received and even won a national gold medal.[3]

As I began to share my stories about Vietnam, I was urged on more than one occasion by friends and colleagues to write down my story. At first I dismissed the idea. Over a thousand books have been published about the Vietnam War. What could I write that would add in any meaningful way to what has already been written? But then I began to reconsider, and it quickly became clear to me that my personal story was so closely intertwined with that of Bill's that it had to be a joint project. I approached Bill with the idea and he quickly agreed.

Once we made the commitment, what followed can only be described as an archeology into our own pasts as each of us began to systematically examine old documents and letters that had been stored away in odd places gathering dust for decades. During his tour of duty,

Bill, a prolific letter writer, had kept up a voluminous correspondence with family and friends and his former mentor Archibald MacLeish. Bill discovered that in nearly all instances the recipients of his correspondence had preserved his letters, including even MacLeish, and this correspondence he has now bequeathed to the MacLeish collection at the Amherst College Library archives.

Our journey of discovery also included several trips to archives and museums. Bill flew down to Texas in the summer of 2018 to discuss the project and to jointly examine the old documents we had. Together we also made a trip back to Fort Sam Houston. The old barracks where 1-A-Os received their basic training, many dating to World Ware I, were still there. It was a touching experience, driving around trying to remember exactly where our barrack was and where we had trained. Bill would suddenly point with excitement: "There it is, that's where ..." The main focus of our trip, however, was the impressive museum dedicated to preserving the history of army medicine. Its official title is US Army Medical Department Museum, but it often goes by the acronym AMEDD.

We wandered through different rooms that correspond to the various wars, showcasing the evolution of army medicine from the very beginning to the present. A vintage Vietnam-era dust-off chopper graced the entrance, which was to my liking. Behind the museum building, in a fenced-off enclosure, we found an extensive collection of antique army ambulances and even a railroad car set up to be a portable hospital. It is an impressive museum and well worth a visit. But one thing jumped out at us right away. There was not one word about the thousands of 1-A-Os who had trained at the fort, men who died and suffered wounds in greater proportion than even their infantry counterparts and who garnered two Congressional Medals of Honor in the Vietnam conflict alone.[4] Not one mention.

This was the beginning of the growing realization of just how far the 1-A-O story has receded, or, as it appeared in the case of the museum, to have been erased. We were perplexed and saddened: Was this intentional or just an oversight? However, something very positive did come from our visit. Using my university credentials,

I had contacted the head archivist, Carlos Alvarado, ahead of time and had requested he pull any documentation concerning basic facts and figures that might help us with our project. How many 1-A-Os trained at Fort Sam Houston? Were class rosters extant? How many served in Vietnam? How many were killed and how many were wounded? Unfortunately, Carlos could neither provide original documents nor answer these questions himself. What he did provide, however, turned out to be a gold mine. He referred us to a doctoral dissertation that he had seen cited in an official military publication. With this citation we were able to obtain "'A Sincere and Meaningful Belief': Legal Conscientious Objection during the Vietnam War," by Dr. Jean Mansavage.[5]

This thorough and altogether excellent study—as it turned out, the only scholarly study we could uncover on the subject—provided some but not all the answers to the questions we were looking for and is referenced in several places in our narratives and essays. Dr. Mansavage had spent weeks doing research at both the National Personnel Records Center in St. Louis, Missouri, the main repository for US Army military records stored on paper, and the National Archives in Maryland, where records from the SSS are housed. She researched both 1-Os (alternative service) and 1-A-Os (medics) during the Vietnam era for her dissertation, but in respect to the latter, many of her facts and figures, such as the number of 1-A-Os who served in Vietnam (about ten thousand), still remain educated guesses since she could locate neither official class rosters, which surely existed at some point, nor other hard records from Echo 4, the special company set up to train 1-A-Os at Fort Sam Houston. What happened to them? Nobody seemed to know, but for our purposes, thanks to her diligent research and informed inferences, at least now we had some basic facts and figures to work with.

Dr. Mansavage, it should be mentioned, now works for the US Air Force as a research historian. I had several very interesting telephone conversations with her, and she also agreed to be interviewed for the "Vietnam on Tape" podcast and to peer-review our initial manuscript.

The following spring (2019) I flew to Wilmington, Delaware, where Bill had moved after retiring the previous year. Together we then took the train to Washington, DC, to do research at the National Archives (Maryland Annex). This proved enlightening for us because an interpretation began to emerge that goes against the conventional wisdom of why Congress, the US military establishment, and the Nixon administration were so keen to replace the draft with an all-voluntary army, which they succeeded in doing in 1973. We concluded that the army's concern for the exponentially growing new breed of 1-A-Os was a determining factor in the decision to abolish the draft. This, in turn, provided a clue as to why the army appears so intent on suppressing, ignoring, disremembering—however one wishes to characterize it—the story in general, a policy clearly on display at the medical museum on the grounds of Fort Sam Houston. Be that as it may, it is a story and a project for another time and place.

Most meaningfully, our journey into the past also included reestablishing contact with old classmates from basic and AIT at Fort Sam, and, in my case, with old crewmates from medevac. Our little group of political 1-A-Os had shared information about ourselves and about other classmates as best we could while in Vietnam through the exchange of letters, the written word being the only means to do so. But once the war was over, with the exception of Bill and me, we went our separate ways and over time drifted out of touch. I also had completely lost contact with my medevac crewmates, with no communication at all in the intervening years. To link up with old comrades after the span of nearly fifty years was a very personal and even emotional event.

Our first reunion was with Fred Ervin, the tall, lanky Black man who had served as class leader in our basic training class. For Fred the example of Jesus was, first and foremost, an example of peace and care for one's fellow human beings, a standard he embodied personally throughout his life, and one that is inspirational. He had made a deep impression by his gentle and unwavering sincerity. Fred had recently retired from a long and successful career as teacher and administrator

Fred Ervin, platoon leader in basic and fellow 1-A-O medic in Vietnam.

in the San Antonio Public School System and was now devoting his full energies to his church, East End Church of God in Christ, located on San Gabriel Street not far from Fort Sam Houston; indeed, many of his parishioners are soldiers at the fort, a fitting turn of events and very meaningful for Fred.

Bill and I sat down with Fred for a couple of hours at his church that summer. We also had along with us Evan Windham, the woman from the Bob Bullock Museum in Austin in charge of producing the podcast. Evan taped our reunion and interviewed Fred about his experiences as a 1-A-O medic in Vietnam, and this interview is featured on one of the podcast episodes. One point that Fred made and emphasized in his interview was that he had been torn between his deeply held belief that it was his duty to serve his country, on the one hand, and his sincere pacifism, on the other. The 1-A-O classi-fication allowed him to reconcile these two convictions—a definitive characteristic for many, if not most, 1-A-O medics.

Andrew Phelan at booksigning. Courtesy of Andrew Phelan.

Next we discovered the whereabouts of Andrew Phelan with the help of an old promotion roster. Subsequently, the three of us enjoyed an extended conference call and then Andy and his wife, the present dean of fine arts at the University of Oklahoma at Norman, paid a visit to my wife and me at the ranch. Interestingly, Bill, Andy, and I all ended up in academia in three different branches of the liberal arts: literature, art history, and German, respectively. For his part, Andy enjoyed a very successful career in the arts and as a published author. He also recently retired as director of the Weizenhoffer Family School of Visual Arts at the University of Oklahoma in Norman.

But, amazingly, unbeknownst to Bill and me, he had written and self-published a book about his own Vietnam experiences, or, more precisely, adventures.[6] He came back with a Bronze Star and a Purple

Heart, and from that fact alone the reader can gather that many of his experiences were also hair-raising. In the book, however, he recounts the trip to the ranch that four of us took and he also reproduces a watercolor he did at the time depicting cows grazing in the distance. His book helped to reawaken a lot of buried memories, corrected others that had gone astray, and contributed meaningfully to my own journey of rediscovery.

Finally, Bill and I also succeeded in discovering the address of the last of the little clique of four political 1-A-Os from our original basic training class at Fort Sam Houston who had come to the ranch on a weekend pass from Fort Sam Houston in 1969, one of the four who prefers to remain anonymous. He had not been able to accept service in Vietnam and used his leave time after AIT to book a flight to Sweden, one of the few countries that then offered asylum to deserters and where he spent the next ten years in exile before returning to the States.[7] Neither Bill, Andy, nor I found any fault with his decision, either at the time or subsequently. Our colleague's decision to go to Sweden underscores, once again, a central characteristic of the Vietnam War that set it apart from all other American wars: one had to decide for himself, and there was no "correct" choice. Astonishingly, nearly a half million Americans deserted during the Vietnam era, more than ten times the number that did so during World War II. Most of them simply kept to the shadows within the United States, but about a thousand, like our colleague, wound up in Sweden. Bill, Andy, and I had chosen to accept our orders for Vietnam, but we respected our friend's decision not to go.[8]

In the spring of 2019 I attended the fiftieth reunion of 15th Medical (Medevac), 1st Air Cavalry Vietnam, which, fortunately for me, was held close by in San Antonio. I had no idea that four of the five crew members from the mission when I was wounded would be in attendance. We had not seen each other or spoken in forty-eight years. When Greg Simpson, now retired as a full bird colonel from the army, saw me, tears welled in his eyes. It was emotional for me as well. Greg said he had never found out what had happened to me. In the

(*Left to right*) Jim Kearney, Greg Simpson, Doc Holiday, and David Weeks at the fiftieth reunion of 15th Medical (Medevac), 1st Air Cavalry Vietnam.

heat of the action, he never understood the full extent of my wounds and had often wondered if, perhaps, I had had to have a leg amputated or something equally extreme. The moment he set our wounded bird down at the aid station, he and the other crew members rushed off to take another bird back into the air to complete the mission. By the time that was completed, I had been whisked away to the 24th Surgical Hospital at Saigon. It was emotional for Greg because he was the sort of commander who cared for his people, and upon seeing me, fit and in one piece after those many years, he was very relieved.

Greg Simpson and I hit it off, and we spent a lot of time together during the three-day reunion. He is an articulate, thoughtful, and conscientious human being. We discussed all sorts of things, including the present political situation. He was not dogmatic, and we felt free to disagree on certain things, but we did so in an atmosphere of mutual respect. He was glad that all the crew members had received Distinguished Flying Crosses for the mission and not just the officers, which, as he confessed, had all too often been the case in Vietnam. Medal inflation had been a serious issue in Vietnam, but it applied almost exclusively to the professional officer corps, who were eager to accumulate citations and cement their reputations in the war. Draftees usually got the short end of the stick in this regard, so when we did garner awards, it was usually well-deserved. That Greg should have been troubled by the short shrift enlisted personnel often received is a testament to his character.

I asked Greg if he would agree to be interviewed for the "Vietnam on Tape" podcast, which was being assembled at this very time by Evan Windham. He consented, and his extensive commentary, especially during the fifth podcast, adds very much to the whole. Indeed, since Greg was not a 1-A-O CO and most of the other people featured on the podcast were, his commentary and point of view provides nice counterpoint and balance. It also offers insight into how the professional officer class regarded 1-A-O medics.

I conclude my narrative with the following remarks: Our story is one of a lifelong friendship forged in the army, but one that has continued to grow and mature beyond the Vietnam experience. Once we committed to writing a book together, Bill and I began by degrees to more fully appreciate the significance and uniqueness of our Vietnam experience, not just in terms of personal narratives but as part of the wider story of that unusual and perhaps unique class of COs, the 1-A-Os, and especially as their legacy relates to Vietnam. In the following chapter, Bill examines the significance of the classification, explores the distinctive challenges it posed for those who applied for the status, and argues that it was a profound loss to the country when it was discontinued in 1973 with the termination of the draft.

Chapter 11

The Conscience
That Was Lost
1-A-O Medics in Vietnam
(*Clamurro*)

The 1-A-O classification for US Army medical corpsmen in the Vietnam War was unique and problematic. Prior to the end of the draft in 1973 as the usual manner of staffing the Army, men had various options for either entering or evading service. There were numerous deferment categories, of course, including exemptions based on medical or physical problems. But there was, first and foremost, the usual and general status of 1-A (available for service). There was also the option to apply to one's draft board for the 1-O, or CO, category. However, there was a third option, distinct from both of these two easily recognizable categories, and this was the category of 1-A-O. The first issue is obvious and has to do with one's MOS. This meant that the man would be a noncombatant soldier, technically within the army but nearly always serving in the medical corps (more than 99 percent of 1-A-Os served as medics), yet with a unique and peculiar status.[1] This was our classification and it determined our status and duties while we were in Vietnam.

The history of the 1-A-O medics, however, has been obscured. When we 1-A-O veterans try to explain it, many people are surprised to hear that it even existed, and many others, when they do learn about it, find it hard to understand. Why did it exist? What sensible young man would opt for such a status? In other words, with the passage of several decades—during which the common idea of anyone's participation in the military has become the view that all military personnel are willing volunteers—the idea that (1) a man or woman would be *involuntarily* conscripted or (2) a person subject to conscription would nonetheless have the option to serve in certain capacities that by law excluded weapons training seems totally illogical, absurd, and baffling.

To put it another way, the truly radical change in recruitment or conscription policy, many years later and now that the heat of the historical moment of the Vietnam conflict has largely faded, brings us to a peculiar conceptual dilemma. Why would a man (and at the time it was, of course, only men) choose to request such a status? The men doing this were, in effect, another kind of volunteer. But we were volunteers in a very unusual way. Was such an act a special kind of patriotism? Or was it a gesture of moral protest, against killing or violence, even while one nonetheless took on a serious responsibility within the military? As the reader can see, the whole idea of 1-A-O is indeed problematic on many levels. It was a peculiar phenomenon at the time—and often an unwanted complexity for the superior officers of the army who had to deal with us—and now, even as the particularities of Vietnam fade into a distant history, it is a story that is hard to process for many people who did not experience or know about it.

At the time it could be argued that during the years prior to the ending of the draft in 1973, the options of the system were largely understood and accepted by most citizens, even though there was considerable opposition to America's involvement in the Vietnam conflict. But with the passage of several decades, and the subtle—and often not sufficiently recognized—changes in how the United States goes into wars and other kinds of military action, many people do not perceive that they have any real obligation to define themselves on certain moral questions, specifically the willingness to engage in combat violence.

The special identity or "role" into which a man placed himself by requesting and then being granted 1-A-O status (1) all but inevitably put him into service as an army medic, and (2) once in the army, he became—like it or not—a kind of moral symbol and an observer. We 1-A-O medics were neither ostentatious nor overly public about our peculiar status. But our presence in a condition of being unarmed was implicitly a commentary on the complexity of war in general and of the Vietnam War in particular.

What I am suggesting, among other things, is that the ending of involuntary conscription and the subsequent elimination of the 1-A-O classification has had the unfortunate effect of taking away from the American public at large the necessity of confronting the moral challenge of taking and articulating a personal stand on the use of military action and violence in the pursuit of foreign policy. Prior to this change, each man (the draft was only for men) had to acquiesce tacitly or object in writing to the usual combatant status. By so doing, he had to confront and think about his moral stance.

Those medics from among all the medical corps personnel who happened to be 1-A-O, as we were, could not make any claim to moral superiority or to being more humane than those who were medics from the regular 1-A classification and who had received weapons training. By agreeing to be in the army in the first instance, we 1-A-Os could never occupy the high moral ground of the traditional and better-known 1-O COs, who eschewed and were granted exemption from all military service. However, it might be pointed out that within the army itself, all medics held a position that gave them a certain moral and humane standing. We were all there in the first instance to heal, not to kill. This was our experience and that of many other medics in Vietnam. Perhaps some of the respect that we were accorded also had to do with the power that we obviously had: we had access to the medicines, instruments, and expertise that the other soldiers knew might mean the difference between life and death.

Once the Vietnam War had ended, and with it the system and threat of involuntary conscription, men no longer had to ponder or scheme how to stay out of actual combat, either by willingly enlisting in one of the other services, or by seeking refuge in a unit of the National Guard, or by some other expedient. I would argue that without the power of coercion resulting from the threat of involuntary conscription, there is no real moral or existential challenge to any individual man with regard to military service. As a result, from the mid-'70s on, the US Army and all the major military branches have basically had to recruit. They have had to sell themselves and entice men and women into their respective service branches. This they have been doing more or less effectively. Thus, although any individual man or woman may choose to enter the service voluntarily and yet still have moral or ideological misgivings about (either) the service that he or she has entered or the military mission in which they take part, no one of them ever has to make an explicit case or justify his or her moral stance.

This post-Vietnam, post-draft situation has far-reaching consequences. From this time onward, the now no-longer-conscripted-citizens army, while still an instrument of foreign policy, is less of a constraint upon the excesses of such policies. In effect, the personnel of the military services now have become an almost unquestioning tool. Other citizens might be reminded or inclined to say, "Thank you for your service." And we often see heart-rending TV ads for men and women who have suffered injury (amputees are frequent images on the TV screen). We may agonize and argue about the need for the adequate medical and psychological care that should be given to these men and women after their time in service. But beyond that we take the military and the participation of the men and women in its various branches for granted.

For this reason, neither the young men of draft-available age nor we others, the now comfortably safe outsiders, are quite so acutely challenged to define and defend our personal moral stance or beliefs. What this means in concrete, practical terms is that we citizens—in any category or of any particular political or moral persuasion, be it religiously based or more loosely secular-ethical in nature—can take any critical position that we desire because we will never be directly challenged to explicitly articulate or argue our moral stance vis-à-vis our participation in military violence or action.

But for our purposes, not only does the 1-A-O classification itself no longer exist, but the memory of it seems also to have vanished, and this, we feel strongly, is unacceptable. Most people still do have a vague awareness of COs who would have had the 1-O status, the classification reserved almost exclusively for men who belonged to historically pacifist sects—the Quakers, Mennonites, Amish, and a handful of others—and whose established beliefs led them to oppose *all* wars and thus precluded them from active participation in the armed forces in any capacity. However, in stark contrast, very few seem to remember what a 1-A-O was, even though the classification existed throughout World War II, Korea, and Vietnam, a span of thirty-three years. In the new reality of an all-volunteer military, such a status or identity makes no sense at all. But in the time prior to 1973 and the end of the draft, and thus the end to the 1-A-O classification, there was a very different awareness. We were there in the war, but we embodied a moral critique of war. This paradox holds a clue to our unique identity, both during our time within the military and now later, as we look back on the history of our participation as veterans. I now sense that the deeply contradictory and paradoxical nature of our role and identity is one of the elements in my own life and experience that I did not fully understand or appreciate at the time but that was to become an issue for me later. Clearly our peculiar status within the US Army was an issue for our colleagues and superiors at the time, although, as I've said, by and large we were often treated with considerable deference, especially by those lifers both inside and outside the medical corps— men who had previously worked with 1-A-O medics in other times and places. But still, we implicitly posed a peculiar dilemma, often in the form of legal limitations on what superior officers could order us to do and also on the decision as to where and how to station us so that our peculiar status would be circumscribed and not become a threat to morale. The reader will find several stories in chapter 4 that illustrate both these situations and predicaments.

This collective amnesia as to the role and significance of 1-A-Os, astonishingly, extends to the army itself. To drive home this point, the army's own otherwise impressive museum of medical history, the US Army Medical Department Museum at Fort Sam Houston in San Antonio, Texas, makes no mention whatsoever of this classification. It is as if it had never existed, and the museum offers not a single word of recognition for the thousands of 1-A-Os who trained at Fort Sam Houston over the years and who perished in the line of duty in World War II, Korea, and Vietnam by the hundreds. This is unacceptable; it is a strange and in fact deeply troubling omission. It strikes us as not merely a negligent oversight but rather as a deliberate suppression of the full story, of the history and sacrifices of those men who were willing to serve but refused to kill, who were willing to aid others and who nonetheless faced the dangers of combat unarmed and defenseless.

I personally was extremely lucky during my time in the army and especially during my fourteen months in Vietnam. I was not wounded nor did I contract any of the common tropical diseases that afflicted many of our comrades. I was also fortunate to be assigned, first, to a tank battalion, 2/34th Armored (of the 25th Division), and later to the 15th Medical Battalion, the clearing-station unit of the 1st Air Cavalry. But my return to civilian life and to my interrupted studies in the graduate school at the University of Washington was not without some uncomfortable challenges. Returning from Vietnam and leaving the army in February of 1971, I was relieved and glad to be back in civilian life, back to graduate school in Seattle. But I was uncomfortable as well. When others—some fellow grad students, a few professors, and some new friends—found out that I had been in the army and in Vietnam, I was occasionally confronted with a curiosity that was critical and at times negative. Even when I explained that I was a noncombatant 1-A-O medic, they still saw me as part of a war that, for the most part, they strongly opposed. It was almost tedious and troublesome for me to try to explain the complexity and mixed feelings of my situation and experiences. I was there, yes, I was part of a military endeavor that I too opposed. But I was willing to help those in need of medical (and often psychological) attention. Perhaps it was simply too complicated and too personal for someone like me, the noncombatant medic, to explain to an outsider. For this reason, ultimately, I tended to downplay my participation and identity within the Vietnam War. In effect, I avoided the issue whenever possible.

Many years later, I have come to wonder if this inclination might also have been a kind of moral cowardice on my part. In more recent years, I have often thought that I should have brought up both my own odd situation within the army and also the implications of the category of my participation, my noncombatant designation. But this was something that I did not do, that I both consciously and unconsciously avoided doing. In effect this avoidance (not total, but still rather routine) could be seen as the attempt to bury the ghosts of Vietnam in my recollection and in what would later be my personal and professional life. Obviously this act of avoidance could not solve the deeper and more intimate problem. I did continue to return to thoughts about Vietnam, more through my poetry than in the form of any extended prose essay or reflection on my own particular experience or on the larger issues that almost any discussion of the Vietnam War tends to bring up.

But now I sense the relevance and urgency of going back to my own story and especially to the now strange-seeming phenomenon of the 1-A-O medic. The whole Vietnam era was a violent, volcanic crucible for America, for our culture and values, as well as for our knowledge of and prudence in world affairs. The presence of the draft and, above all, the existence of the 1-A-O option was a deeply meaningful element of the challenge of moral self-definition that so many men faced. In addition, because multitudes faced and went through it, this meant that our families and friends, the close relationships that we had at the time, also shared—if more vicariously—this moral challenge.

In conclusion, it seems to us that, quite apart from rendering due respect and acknowledgment to the men of our status who served—those who died there as well as those who survived—it is incumbent upon us to keep alive the memory of the unique importance of that peculiar, paradoxical identity that we and our fellow 1-A-Os shared within the army. We were men willing to serve on the frontlines, on the one hand, but men who embodied an implicit critique of war and violence, on the other. Thus, in recovering this history, we are hoping to shine a necessary light on a valuable consciousness and conscience that has been lost.

A Final Word

(*Kearney and Clamurro*)

In 1969, when confronted with the draft and service in a war we had come to detest, we felt torn between a duty to serve and a duty to conscience. The 1-A-O classification, originally authorized by the Selective Service Act of 1940 and accepted by the US Army until the termination of the draft in 1973, permitted us to reconcile these opposing challenges, and for this we were grateful. Fifty years later this need has been replaced by an overwhelming sense that we have a debt to repay, a debt first and foremost to the secular humanistic tradition and value system that we both embraced during our formative years, and which sustained us, then as now—a tradition that gave us the tools to think critically, the conscience to act compassionately, and the determination to take a stand for the better instincts of humankind. This book represents our homage to that tradition.

Editing the Thread (June–July 2022)

The two of us are reading slowly through
the text, a narrative of what has lived
so many years ago, the actions, what
we saw and heard, that somehow we survived.

We read aloud, stop to replace a word
or change the shape or rhythm of a phrase.
but we are also searching memories
of times inscribed by violence and fear.

I can't escape the sense that recollection
means that once again we collect
those fragments of our past, in fact a war,
intensely real yet, fading with the years.

We pore with keen attention, often pause,
to weigh the words, this draft we need to end,
while outside the silences and sounds
of a peaceful Texas ranch enfold us

as we read and search, retracing
the deep, enduring fabric of our bond.

Appendixes

Appendix 1. Witness Statement of James Kearney, Houston, Texas, April 4, 1969

WITNESS STATEMENT
(AR 195-10 - TB PMG 3)

PLACE Houston, Texas	DATE 4 Apr 69	TIME 1400 hrs	FILE NUMBER

LAST NAME, FIRST NAME, MIDDLE NAME KEARNEY, James Charles	SOCIAL SECURITY ACCOUNT NO.	GRADE

ORGANIZATION OR ADDRESS U. S. Armed Forces Examining and Entrance Station, 701 San Jacinto Street, Houston, Texas

SWORN STATEMENT

I, James Charles Kearney , WANT TO MAKE THE FOLLOWING STATEMENT UNDER OATH

Q. Mr. Kearney, before we proceed, I should like to explain to you that this interview offers an advantage to you as well as the Army. The technical name for this type of interview is Selective Service Registrant Subject Interview and results from, and is intended to afford you the opportunity to furnish an explanation of your qualification of DD Form 98, Armed Forces Security Questionnaire, and DD Form 398, Statement of Personal History, and to furnish any additional information which may be useful in making a determination of your case. Although you are not suspected or accused of any offense, the Department of the Army is concerned by your qualification and must necessarily assure itself of the loyalty and dependability of its present and future members. Therefore, the forms should not be interpreted as constituting an abridgement of your rights and privileges. Do you understand the foregoing?
A. Yes.--
Q. The Department of the Army desires that this interview be conducted under oath. Are you willing at this time to be interviewed under oath?
A. Yes.--
Q. Please stand and raise your right hand. Do you swear or affirm that the information you are about to give is the truth, the whole truth, and nothing but the truth, so help you God?
A. I do.--
Q. Please state your full name, address, date and place of birth, occupation and place of employment, and Social Security Number.
A. James Charles Kearney. I reside at Route 3, Weimar, Texas. I was born on 20 February 1946, at Columbus, Texas. I am a student at the University of Texas, Austin, Texas. My Social Security Number is .-------------------------------------
Q. Are you now or have you ever been known by any other name or nickname, or have there been changes in your name?
A. I have a nickname of Jim for James.--
Q. Mr. Kearney, I have here your DD Form 98, Armed Forces Security Questionnaire, and your DD Form 398, Statement of Personal History, both dated 3 April 1969, to which you have affixed your signature. Do you recognize these forms, their entries, and are these your signatures?
A. Yes, those are the forms I filled out and signed.--------------------------------
Q. Please examine these forms - do you wish to make any additions to, deletions of, or changes to the information on these forms at this time?
A. No.--
Q. Mr. Kearney, you have indicated an association with the Students For Democratic Society (SDS), is that correct?
A. Yes.--
Q. When and where have you attended meetings of the Students For Democratic Society?
A. During the Spring of 1968, I attended approximately three protest rallies, in Austin, Texas, sponsored either by the Students For Democratic Society or the

EXHIBIT	INITIALS OF PERSON MAKING STATEMENT *JCK*	PAGE 1 OF 4 PAGES

*ADDITIONAL PAGES MUST CONTAIN THE HEADING "STATEMENT OF___ TAKEN AT___ DATED___ CONTINUED."
THE BOTTOM OF EACH ADDITIONAL PAGE MUST BEAR THE INITIALS OF THE PERSON MAKING THE STATEMENT AND
BE INITIALED AS "PAGE___OF___PAGES." WHEN ADDITIONAL PAGES ARE UTILIZED, THE BACK OF PAGE 1 WILL
BE LINED OUT, AND THE STATEMENT WILL BE CONCLUDED ON THE REVERSE SIDE OF ANOTHER COPY OF THIS FORM.*

DA FORM 2823
1 JAN 68

212   Appendixes

"Statement of James Charles Kearney Taken at Houston, Texas, Dated 4 April 1969
Continued"

A. University Committee to End the War in Viet Nam. During the period of 28 to
30 March 1969, I attended the National Convenction of the Students For Democratic
Society at Austin, Texas.---
Q. Why did you attend these meetings?
A. I attended the National Convention of the Students For a Democratic Society for
several reasons. The chief of these was that I had for some time contemplated joining
some organization through which on the basis of my opinions, I could take an active
part in political affairs. The Students For Democratic Society was one organization
among others that I thought of joining. Since the Students For Democratic Society
was having its National Convention in Austin, Texas, I decided to attend as a guest
so as to acquaint myself first hand with their views and see how these corresponded
with my own. This I did.---
Q. At the time you attended these meetings, were you aware that the Students For
Democratic Society was considered by the US Government to be an organization that was
controlled or strongly influenced by individuals or foreign governments that are
hostile toward the American way of life?
A. No.--
Q. Are you presently a member or have you been a member and what are your intentions
concerning future association with the Students For Democratic Society?
A. I have never been a member of the Students For Democratic Society and at the present
do not plan to become a member.---
Q. What personal services or monetary contribution have you made to the Students For
Democratic Society?
A. I have made no monetary contribution nor contributed personal services to the
Students For Democratic Society. I did pay a $5.00 registration fee for attendance
at the convention, and have purchased approximately $5.00 in Students For Democratic
Society Publications.---
Q. Mr. Dearney, would you further clearify your remark in Section IV, DD Form 98,
concerning the publication you mentioned and what you did with these publications?
A. At this convention there were several other organizations other than the Students
For Democratic Society, some of which might perhaps be considered "Communistic." They
were all very industriously engaged in handing out their propaganda. As it is my
conviction that one should examine the evidence before reaching a decision, I collect-
ed from one and all without thereby implying that I agree or disagree with any of
them. It was purely a fact finding thing. At this time, all of this material is still
in my possession. After I have finished going through it, I intend to send some of it
to my friends with whom I correspond regularly, as it is customary for us to exchange
ideas, opinions, and printed materials.--
Q. Mr. Kearney, would you explain the circumstances concerning your employment with
Karl Kübler Construction Firm in Germany.
A. I spent the whole summer of 1966 in Europe. Most of this time (2 months) was spent
in Goeppingen, West Germany, where I was employed as a construction worker for Karl
Kübler Construction Firm. The other month I spent in travelling. I travelled to
Austria, through Switzerland to Geneva, from there to Paris and from Paris to England,

Page _2_ of _4_ Pages

"Statement of James Charles Kearney Taken at Houston, Texas Dated 4 April 1969
Continued"

A. where I spent my last week. I travelled by hitchhiking and stayed in youth
hotels where one has the opportunity of meeting young people from many lands and
exchanging views with them. I went to Europe as a result of the conviction that time
spent in travel is at least as educational as time spent in school. One of the best
ways to understand one's own culture, country, or self is to see it in perspective.
This conviction plus the fact that I had studied the German language and German
history prompted me to want to see Germany and Europe.-------------------------------
Q. Do you or would you support any individual or organization which advocates the
overthrow of our constitutional government, or which has adopted the policy of advocat-
ing or approving the commission of acts of force or violence to deny other persons
their rights under the Constitution of the United States?
A. No.---
Q. Do you or would you support any organization or individual which seeks to alter the
form of government of the United States by acts of force, violence or other unconstitu-
tional means?
A. No.---
Q. Do you have any objections to being inducted into the US Armed Forces under the
current laws governing the induction of personnel for the US Armed Forces?
A. In principal, I profoundly disagree to being inducted into the US Armed Services
because, I am thoroughly and unequivocally opposed to the present war in Viet Nam ,
and under present law I cannot become a Conscientious Objector on other than religous
grounds. Since the alternative is three years in prison, I will however probably accept
induction. This government together with the other allied powers of World War II
tried and put to death Germans for not following their consciousnesses instead of
their leaders. Yet when Americans do follow their consciousnesses instead of their
leaders they are thrown in jail. This seems to me to show some hypocracy.------------
Q. If Inducted, will you serve to the best of your ability and obey the laws govern-
ing the members of the United States Armed Forces?
A. At this time, I can't honestly say what I will or won't do. I just don't know.---
Q. Do you believe in and support the Constitution of the United States Government?
A. Yes.--
Q. Do you feel that you owe allegiance and loyalty to the United States?
A. Yes.------------------------------------ ------------------------------------
Q. Are you willing to serve the United States against any and all enemies, without
exception?
A. Yes.--

Page _3_ of _4_ Pages

STATEMENT (Continued)

Q. Are you willing to sign a sworn statement on the contents of this interview?
A. Yes --
Q. Is there anything you would like to add to this interview?
A. Yes, in connection with the question as to whether I knew that the Students For
Democratic Society was considered subversive by the Defense Department, my answer
needs some clarification. I had earlier (on 15 March 1969) filled out a DD Form 98
upon application for a ROTC Program. At that time, the Students For Democratic Society
was not on the list of subversive organizations. It has apparently only recently been
added. ---
//////////////////////////////////END OF STATEMENT///////////////////////////////////////

AFFIDAVIT

I, _James Charles Kearney_ HAVE READ OR HAVE HAD READ TO ME THIS STATE-
MENT WHICH BEGINS ON PAGE 1 AND ENDS ON PAGE __4__. I FULLY UNDERSTAND THE CONTENTS OF THE ENTIRE STATEMENT
MADE BY ME. THE STATEMENT IS TRUE. I HAVE INITIALED ALL CORRECTIONS AND HAVE INITIALED THE BOTTOM OF EACH PAGE
CONTAINING THE STATEMENT. I HAVE MADE THIS STATEMENT FREELY WITHOUT HOPE OF BENEFIT OR REWARD, WITHOUT THREAT
OF PUNISHMENT, AND WITHOUT COERCION, UNLAWFUL INFLUENCE, OR UNLAWFUL INDUCEMENT.

James Charles Kearney
(Signature of Person Making Statement)

WITNESSES:

Barbara J. Dye _Barbara J. Dye_

Subscribed and sworn to before me, a person authorized by law
to administer oaths, this __4__ day of __April__, 19 _69_
at __Houston, Texas__

ORGANIZATION OR ADDRESS

Armed Forces Examining and Entrance Station
Houston, Texas

Charles F. Ray
(Signature of Person Administering Oath)
CHARLES F. RAY
Special Agent   USAINTC
(Typed Name of Person Administering Oath)

ORGANIZATION OR ADDRESS

Art 136(b) UCMJ
(Authority To Administer Oaths)

INITIALS OF PERSON MAKING STATEMENT

PAGE 4 OF 4 PAGES

Appendix 2. Gregory Robertson to
S. K. Seymour Jr., May 17, 1969

May 17, 1969

Mr. S. K. Seymour, Jr.   Re: Mr. Jim Kearney
Chairman, Draft Board #44   2103 Nueces
603 Travis   Austin, Texas 78705
Columbus, Texas 78934

Dear Sam K.:

We have within our church two sons: a conscientious participator in
military service and a conscientious objector to war. My personal
convictions, grounded in the historic stance of the church and the
scriptures, compels me to support both of these sons in making a
conscientious decision concerning military service. My support of
Mr. Jim Kearney is essentially the same as that which I give to every
young man in making his own decision about participation in war.
Those who decide that, in Christian conscience, they should enter the
Armed Forces (e.g. Lt. John Kearney, Jim's brother) have my support
and my prayers. But each man must make his own choice. And if he
conscientiously objects to war, as in the case of Mr. Jim Kearney, then
he will receive my council concerning his rights in this respect,
assistance in bringing his claim before the draft board, and support
in securing recognition of those rights. My stance, briefly stated,
reaffirms the official position of the United Methodist Church.

> We (the United Methodist Church) recognize the right of
> the individual to answer the call of his government accord-
> ing to the dictates of his Christian conscience. Believing
> that government rests upon the support of its conscientious
> citizens, it holds within its fellowship those who sincerely
> differ as to the Christian's duty in regard to military
> service. We ask and claim exemption by legal processes from
> all forms of military preparation or service for all reli-
> gious conscientious objectors, as for those of the historic
> peace churches. (Paragraph 96, 1968 Book of Discipline,
> The United Methodist Church)

After several hours of extended conversation with Jim Kearney, I am
convinced that his belief in God and his convictions as how to serve
best the cause of humanity and of his country are credible. Furthermore, it has been my observation during the past three years that I
have known Jim as his pastor, that his beliefs and his acts are not
in conflict. Believing that war is immoral, Jim chooses not to fire
a gun or drop a bomb; but he is willing to serve what he believes to
be the best interests of his country and of humanity by relieving the
suffering of wounded men as a non-combatant (1-A-O) in medical service
duty. I can not call this decision dishonorable or cowardly. Jim
did not come to this decision without a deep struggle of conscience
and mind. Sensitive to the effect that this decision would have upon
his parents and his brother, Jim still could not bring himself to
affirm a stand that would violate his own conscience.

It is my ardent hope that you will recognize the right of both sons
within our church: the right of the conscientious participant and
the right of the conscientious objector. For it is upon both these
sons that our nation's hope and future rests.

Sincerely yours,

Gregory Robertson

GR:dr

cc: Mr. Jim Kearney

Endnotes

Prologue

1. SSS Form 150, Sections A and B; Records Relating to Conscientious Objectors, Box 1; Selective Service System Files, Record Group 147 (RG 147); National Archives at College Park, MD (NACP). The SSS Form 150 was a standard form for requesting conscientious objector status that was available upon request from every draft board in the country. It was authorized by the Selective Service Act of 1940 and continued to be used in the same form and with the same wording until the draft was abolished in 1973. For a discussion of the document and how it was used, see Jean Anne Mansavage, "'A Sincere and Meaningful Belief': Legal Conscientious Objection during the Vietnam War," PhD dissertation, Texas A&M University, 2000, 67–69.

Chapter 1

1. "Citizens' Military Training Camp," Wikipedia, accessed June 30, 2019, https://en.wikipedia.org/wiki/Citizens%27_Military_Training_Camp.
2. "Pinky Wilson and the Aggie War Hymn," Museum of the American GI, accessed March 22, 2023, https://americangimuseum.org/collections/exhibits/pinky-wilson-and-the-aggie-war-hymn/.
3. Bertrand Russell, *Has Man a Future?* (New York: Simon and Schuster, 1962).
4. Bertrand Russell, *Freedom and Organization 1814–1914* (London: George Allen & Unwin, 1934).
5. Hans Kohn, *The Idea of Nationalism* (New York: Collier Books, 1944).
6. For the evolution of student activism at the University of Texas, see Beverly Burr, "History of Student Activism at the University of Texas at Austin (1960–1988)" (master's thesis, University of Texas at Austin, 1988).
7. Alice Embree and Thorne Dreyer still maintain a blog for *The Rag* termed the "New Journalism Project." (theragblog.com). They have also published a book about the heyday of the paper: *Celebrating the Rag: Austin's Iconic Underground Newspaper* (Austin: New Journalism Project, 2016).
8. Bob Dylan, "The Times They Are a-Changin'," track 1, side 1 on *The Times They Are a-Changin'*, Columbia Records, 1964.

9. *The Rag*, April 24, 1967, p. 10.

10. Edwin Reischauer, *Beyond Vietnam: The United States and Asia* (New York: Random House, 1967); J. William Fulbright, *The Arrogance of Power* (New York: Random House, 1966).

11. *The Fog of War: Eleven Lessons from the Life of Robert S. McNamara,* directed by Errol Morris, documentary film, Sony Pictures Classics, 2003.

12. These lyrics from the song "I-Feel-Like-I'm-Fixin'-to-Die," by Country Joe and the Fish, emerged as one of the iconic protest songs of the 1960s. The author had the privilege of meeting Country Joe (Joseph Allen McDonald) at a Vietnam War Summit sponsored by the University of Texas in April 2014.

13. Robert Krim, "SDS Conference Starts in Austin," special edition, *Harvard Crimson*, March 28, 1969.

14. "COINTELPRO," *Wikipedia*, accessed September 12, 2019, https://en.wikipedia.org/wiki/COINTELPRO; Betty Medsger, *The Burglary: The Discovery of J. Edgar Hoover's Secret FBI* (New York: Alfred Knopf, 2014).

15. For more on COINTELPRO see Nelson Blackstock, *Cointelpro: The FBI's Secret War on Political Freedom*, 3rd ed. (New York: Pathfinder Press, 1988).

16. The files are in the Briscoe Center for American History Studies at the University of Texas at Austin.

17. "Hypothetical Conscientious Objector Case Forwarded to the National Headquarters for Review," Lieutenant Colonel Mueller; Memorandum to all State Directors by the General Counsel of the SSS July 1971; From: Conscientious Objector Branch Manager; Subject: Basis in fact for denying a registrant's claim for a conscientious objector classification; Conscientious Objectors, Box 1; RG 147; NACP.

18. SSS Form 150; Conscientious Objectors, Box 1; RG 147; NACP.

19. Mansavage, "Sincere and Meaningful Belief."

20. SSS Form 150; Conscientious Objectors, Box 1; RG 147; NACP.

21. Mansavage, "Sincere and Meaningful Belief," 197. She states, "Colonel Charles Pixlcy, commander of the U.S. Army Medical Training Center, Fort Sam Houston, Texas, 1967–1972, and other sources state that between 98 and 99 percent of conscientious objectors in the Army become medical aidmen."

Chapter 2

1. "Oaths of Enlistment and Oaths of Office," U.S. Army Center of Military History website, https://history.army.mil/faq/oaths.html.
2. Mansavage, "Sincere and Meaningful Belief."
3. Andrew L. Phelan, *Free: Letters and Remembrances from Vietnam with a Selection of Civil War Letters written by Eugene Kingman* (Norman, OK: Quail Creek Editions, 2006).
4. Nicholas C. Chriss, "380 Conscientious Objectors Train as Medics: Echo 4 Co. at Ft. Sam Houston Is the Most Unorthodox Unit in the US Army," *Los Angeles Times-Washington Post News Service*, 1969.

Chapter 3

1. Phelan, *Free*, 43.
2. "Long Binh Post," Wikipedia, accessed March 23, 2023, https://en.wikipedia.org/wiki/Long_Binh_Post.
3. "Long Binh Post," Wikipedia.
4. For a recent national article on this see Lukasz Kamienski, "The Drugs That Built a Super Soldier during the Vietnam War," *Atlantic Magazine*, April 8, 2016.
5. William H. Clamurro, *The Vietnam Typescript* (Emporia, KS: Bluestem Press, 2018).
6. Clamurro, *Vietnam Typescript*.
7. SP 4 Frank Morris, "Aidman Is Comedian Is Bard: This Grouch Leaves Marks," *Tropic Lightning News*, n.d.

Chapter 4

1. Clamurro, *Vietnam Typescript*.

Chapter 5

1. "Kent State Shootings," Wikipedia, accessed September 3, 2019, https://en.wikipedia.org/wiki/Kent_State_shootings.
2. Clamurro, *Vietnam Typescript*.
3. Thich Nhat Hanh, *Vietnam: Lotus in a Sea of Fire; A Buddhist Proposal for Peace* (New York: Hill and Wang, 1967), 63.

Chapter 6

1. Phelan, *Free*.
2. Clamurro, *Vietnam Typescript*.

Chapter 7

1. Binyamin Appelbaum, *The Economists' Hour: False Prophets, Free Markets, and the Fracture of Society* (New York: Little, Brown, 2019), 45.

Chapter 8

1. For more on dust-off and medevac see John L. Cook, *Rescue under Fire: The Story of Dust Off in Vietnam* (Atglen, PA: Schiffer, 1998); Michael J. Novosel, *Dustoff: The Memoir of an Army Aviator* (Novato, CA: Presidio, 2003); and Glenn M. Williams, *So Others Might Live* (Mukilteo, WA: WinePress, 1998).
2. Clamurro, *Vietnam Typescript*.

Chapter 9

1. Bao Ninh was a North Vietnamese soldier who survived twelve years of war. His memoir, *The Sorrow of War: A Novel of North Vietnam* ([Hanoi: Writers' Association Publishing House, 1991]; reprint, ed. Frank Palmos, trans. Phan Thanh Hao, [New York: Pantheon Books, 1995]) is to my mind one of the most powerful antiwar narratives ever written. He uses the phrase "engaging the Americans by their belt loops" in several places to describe NVA strategy. By getting and staying as close as possible to the Americans, they could avoid the devasting effect of artillery or helicopter gunships.
2. Clamurro, *Vietnam Typescript*.

Chapter 10

1. Clamurro, *Vietnam Typescript*.
2. For access to the podcast see: https://www.thestoryoftexas.com/discover/podcast/vietnam-on-tape.
3. The podcast "Vietnam on Tape" won a TAMMIE award from the Texas Association of Museums and the Gold MUSE Award for the best podcast produced by a museum in the United States from the American Association of Museums for the year 2019.

4. This is, admittedly, a guess because the army did not keep specific statistics on 1-A-Os such as the number of deaths, number of awards, and so on. However, Mansavage "Sincere and Meaningful Belief," 210, points out that while 1-A-Os accounted for only about .75 percent of the 1.95 million men inducted into the army during the Vietnam War, they accounted for 1.29 per cent of the recipients of the Congressional Medal of Honor, and the majority of Medals of Honor were awarded posthumously. These citations do list 1-A-O status. From this, much can be inferred.

5. Mansavage, "Sincere and Meaningful Belief."

6. Phelan, *Free.*

7. Desertion was, and is, a much more serious offense than draft evasion and, on the books at least, can be punished with the firing squad. To desert, then, was a serious decision that could have lifelong consequences even without a firing squad.

8. One needs to make a clear distinction between draft evaders and deserters. A draft evader was someone who ignored his induction order or, like Mohmmed Ali, refused to take the oath of allegiance during the induction ceremony. A deserter was one who fled military service after induction. Draft evaders faced punishment in civilian courts, and the punishment was usually a prison term of two or three years. Deserters, on the other hand, had to appear before military tribunals, and the punishments were usually much harsher, and in certain circumstances could include the firing squad. President Gerald Ford signed a proclamation in 1974 that granted conditional amnesty to draft evaders, provided they work in a public service job for up to two years. Those who had evaded the draft by leaving the country were not eligible for a conditional pardon. President Carter, in fulfillment of a campaign pledge, expanded amnesty to all draft evaders with Proclamation 4483 on January 21, 1977. Amnesty was never granted to deserters, but few were prosecuted after 1973. Thus those deserters who returned to the United States after many years abroad in Sweden and other places, such as our basic training classmate, still have the threat of prosecution hanging over their heads. ("Proclamation 4483," Wikipedia, accessed April 2, 2023, https://en.wikipedia.org/wiki/Proclamation_4483.)

Chapter 11

1. Mansavage, "Sincere and Meaningful Belief," 197.

Bibliography

1-A-O Medics in Vietnam

Archives

Military Personnel Records, National Personnel Records Center, St. Louis, MO.

Records Relating to Conscientious Objectors, Box 1; Selective Service System Files, Record Group 147; National Archives at College Park, MD.

US Army Medical Department Museum Archives (AMEDD) at Fort Sam Houston, San Antonio, TX; Carlos Alvarado, chief archivist.

Books and articles

Barnes, Dick. "Growing Hard Line Seen on Objector Deferments." *Anniston Star* (Anniston, AL), June 12, 1968.

Center on Conscience and War. *The Reporter for Conscience' Sake*. (A publication providing information for those applying for conscientious objector status in 1967 and for many years thereafter. More recent archives of the newsletter can be found online at https://centeronconscience.org/the-reporter/.)

Chriss, Nicholas C. "380 Conscientious Objectors Train as Medics: Echo 4 Co. at Ft. Sam Houston Is the Most Unorthodox Company in the US Army." *Los Angeles Times-Washington Post News Service*, 1969.

Clamurro, William H. *The Vietnam Typescript*. Emporia, KS: Bluestem Press, 2018.

Donahey, Ron. *Vietnam Combat Medic: A CO in the Central Highlands*. Self-published, Deeds Publishing, 2018. (Like Desmond Doss in WWII, Donahey is a Seventh-Day Adventist, as were many 1-A-O medics.)

"The Draft: Soldiers without Arms." *Time Magazine*, October 28, 1966.

Goldberger, Peter, letter to the editor. "War Objector Status." *New York Times*, October 8, 1968.

Maffre, Jack. "It's Hard to Qualify." *Washington Post*, October 16, 1966.

"Medic in Vietnam: War Hater Excels at most Dangerous Job." *Los Angeles Times*, September 22, 1968.

Merron, Rick. "A Conscientious Objector Becomes a Hero to Comrades without Gun at Dak To." *Washington Post*, November 19, 1967.

Mills, Randy K. *Troubled Hero: A Medal of Honor, Vietnam, and the War at Home*. Bloomington: Indiana University Press, 2006. (Story of Kenneth Kays, denied CO status only to enlist if promised medical training. Didn't carry a weapon, MOH awardee, and later a suicide.)

Phelan, Andrew L. *Free: Letters and Remembrances from Vietnam with a Selection of Civil War Letters written by Eugene Kingman*. Norman, OK: Quail Creek Editions, 2006. (Andrew was a classmate of Bill Clamurro and Jim Kearney in basic training at Fort Sam Houston, Texas.)

Robinson, Douglas. "Conscientious Objectors Win Respect on Vietnam Battlefields." *New York Times*, October 8, 1968.

Sharbutt, Jack. "Pacifist Kills to Save a Buddy." *Chicago Tribune*, May 2, 1969.

Sherman, Ben. *Medic! The Story of a CO in the Vietnam War*. New York: Ballantine, 2002. (Untrustworthy, opens with a bizarre story of being assigned to a graves registration unit, which is not a medical corps function).

Trimborn, Harry. "Conscientious Objectors Show Courage in Vietnam Action." *Washington Post*, June 23, 1969.

Dissertation

Mansavage, Jean Anne. "'A Sincere and Meaningful Belief': Legal Conscientious Objection during the Vietnam War." PhD dissertation, Texas A&M University, 2000.

Podcast

Kearney, James. "Vietnam on Tape." 5 episodes, edited by Evan Windham, December 13, 2019, through January 10, 2020. Season 2 of *Texas Story Podcast*, produced by the Bullock Museum, Austin, TX. https://www.thestoryoftexas.com/discover/podcast/vietnam-on-tape. (A fifty-year-old cassette recording unravels a Vietnam veteran's story of disappearing history, life-long friendship, and reconnection.)

Combat Medics in Vietnam in General

Dingman, C. Michael. *Unlikely Warrior: Memoirs of a Vietnam Combat Medic*. Maitland, FL: Xulon, 2014.

Roberson, Cliff. *Vietnam Medic: Field Journal*. Ukiah, CA: CaeSaR Books, 2011.

1-A-O Medics in World War II

Doss, Frances M. *Desmond Doss: Conscientious Objector*. Nampa, ID: Pacific Press, 2005.

"Medal of Honor Recipient PFC Desmond Doss." *AMEDD Historian* (Army Medical Department Center of History and Heritage), no. 1, Winter 2013.

University of Texas and the Vietnam War

Ashworth, Kenneth. *Horns of a Dilemma: Coping with Politics at the University of Texas*. Austin: University of Texas Press, 2011.

Burr, Beverly. "History of Student Activism at the University of Texas at Austin (1960–1988)." Master's thesis, University of Texas, 1988.

Davis, Steven L. "A Texas Oasis." In *Texas Literary Outlaws: Six Writers in the Sixties and Beyond*, 25–38. Fort Worth: Texas Christian University Press, 2004.

Dreyer, Thorne. "The Spies of Texas." *Texas Observer*, November 17, 2006.

Embree, Alice, and Thorne Dreyer. *Celebrating the Rag: Austin's Iconic Underground Newspaper*. Austin: New Journalism Project, 2016.

"Freedom and Order at UT." *Texas Observer*, May 12, 1967, pp. 1–4.

Kearney, James, "Central Texas German's Tale." *Austin American Statesman*, March 4, 2012.

Krim, Robert. "SDS Conference Starts in Austin." Special edition, *Harvard Crimson*, March 28, 1969.

Larsen, Roy. Letter to "The Firing Line." *Daily Texan*, March 23, 1969.

Leamer, Laurence. *The Paper Revolutionaries: The Rise of the Underground Press*. New York: Simon and Schuster, 1972.

Olan, Susan Torian. *The Rag: A Study in Underground Journalism*. Master's thesis, University of Texas at Austin, 1981.

Richards, Dave. *Once Upon a Time in Texas: A Liberal in the Lone Star State*. Austin: University of Texas Press, 2002.

Conscientious Objection in General

Anderson, Richard C. *Peace Was in Their Hearts*. Philadelphia: Herald, 1994.

Applebaum, Benjamin. *The Economists' Hour: False Prophets, Free Markets, and the Fracture of Society*. New York: Little, Brown, 2019.

Ballou, Adin. *Christian Non-resistance in All Its Important Bearings*. 1846. Reprint Universal Peace Union, 1910; reprint Oberlin, Ohio, 2010.

Brock, Peter. *Against the Draft: Essays on Conscientious Objection from the Radical Reformation to the Second World War*. Toronto: University of Toronto Press, 2006.

Brock, Peter. *Pacifism in the United States: From the Colonial Era to the First World War*. Princeton, NJ: Princeton University Press, 1968.

Brock, Peter. *These Strange Criminals: An Anthology of Prison Memoirs by Conscientious Objectors from the Great War to the Cold*. Toronto: University of Toronto Press, 2004.

Camus, Albert. *Neither Victims nor Executioners*. New York: War Resisters League reprint, N.D.

Chelčický, Petr. *The Net of Faith: The Corruption of the Church, Caused by Its Fusion and Confusion with Temporal Power*. Compiled by Tom Lock. Translated by Enrico C. S. Molnár. n.p.: Audio Enlightenment, 2017.

Cooney, Robert, and Helen Michalowski. *The Power of the People: Active Nonviolence in the United States*. Culver City, CA: Peace Press, 1977.

Dasenbrock, J. Henry. *To the Beat of a Different Drummer*. Winona, MN: Northland Press of Winona, 1989.

Eberle, Donald. "The Plain Mennonite Face of the World War One Conscientious Objector." *Journal of Amish and Plain Anabaptist Studies*, 3 no. 2 (2015): 175–201.

Ferber, Michael, and Staughton Lynd. *The Resistance*. Boston: Beacon, 1971.

Gandhi, M.K. *Non-Violent Resistance*. New York: Schocken Books, 1951.

Green, Martin. *The Origins of Nonviolence: Tolstoy and Ghandi in Their Historical Settings*. University Park: Pennsylvania State University Press, 1986.

Guinan, Edward. *Peace and Nonviolence*. New York: Paulist, 1973.

Hershberger, Guy. *War, Peace and Nonresistance*. Scottsdale, PA: Herald, 1944.

Hobhouse, Mrs. Henry. *I Appeal unto Ceasar: The Case of the Conscientious Objector*. Edinburg: R&R Clark, 1916. Reprint, London: Forgotten Books, 2015.

Howard, Michael. *War and the Liberal Conscience*. New Brunswick, NJ: Rutgers University Press, 1978.

Kearney, James. "A Short History of Pacifism in the Western Tradition as It Relates to 1-A-O Conscientious Objectors in Vietnam." Essay in *Festschrift for Janet Swaffar*, forthcoming.

Keim, Albert N. *The CPS Story: An Illustrated History of Civilian Public Service*. Intercourse, PA: Good Books, 1990.

Keim, Albert N., and Grant Stoltzfus. *The Politics of Conscience: The Historic Peace Churches and America at War, 1917–1955*. Scottdale, PA: Herald, 1988.

Kellogg, Walter Guest. *The Conscientious Objector*. New York: Boni and Liveright, 1919.

King, Martin Luther, Jr. *Stride toward Freedom*. New York: Harper and Row, 1958.

Kohn, Hans. *The Idea of Nationalism*. New York: Collier Books, 1944.

Kohn, Stephen M. *Jailed for Peace: The History of American Draft Law Violators, 1655–1985*. New York: Praeger, 1986.

Lynd, Staughton. *Nonviolence in America: A Documentary History*. Indianapolis: Bobbs-Merrill, 1966.

Miller, William Robert. *Nonviolence: A Christian Interpretation*. New York: Schocken Books, 1966.

Muste, Abraham J. *Non-Violence in an Aggressive World*. New York: Harper, 1972.

Russell, Bertrand. *Has Man a Future?* New York: Simon and Schuster, 1962.

Tolstoy, Leo. *The Kingdom of God Is Within You*. Trans. Constance Garnett. Foreword by Martin Green. Lincoln: University of Nebraska Press, 1984.

Tracy, James. *Direct Action: Radical Pacifism from the Union Eight to the Chicago Seven*. Chicago: University of Chicago Press, 1996.

Van den Dungen, Peter. *The Conquest of Violence: An Essay on War and Revolution*. London: Pluto, 1989.

Wilhelm, Paul A. *Civilian Public Servants*. Washington, DC: NISBCO, 1994.

Will, Herman. *A Will for Peace*. Washington, DC: General Board of Church and Society, 1984.

Wittner, Lawrence S. *Rebels against War: The American Peace Movement, 1933–1983*. Philadelphia, PA: Temple University Press, 1984.

Zahn, Gordon C. *War, Conscience, and Dissent*. New York: Hawthorn Books, 1967.

Zinn, Howard. *A People's History of the United States*. New York: Harper Collins, 1980.

Further Reading

Appelbaum, Binyamin. *The Economists' Hour: False Prophets, Free Markets, and the Fracture of Society*. New York: Little, Brown, 2019.

Blackstock, Nelson. *Cointelpro: The FBI's Secret War on Political Freedom*. 3rd ed. New York: Pathfinder Press, 1988.

Cook, John L. *Rescue under Fire: The Story of Dust Off in Vietnam*. Atglen, PA: Schiffer, 1998.

Fulbright, J. William. *The Arrogance of Power*. New York: Random House, 1966.

Hanh, Thich Nhat. *Vietnam: Lotus in a Sea of Fire; A Buddhist Proposal for Peace*. New York: Hill and Wang, 1967.

Ninh, Bao. *The Sorrow of War: A Novel of North Vietnam*. Hanoi: Writers' Association Publishing House, 1991. Reprint, ed. Frank Palmos, trans. Phan Thanh Hao, New York: Pantheon Books, 1995.

Novosel, Michael J. *Dustoff: The Memoir of an Army Aviator*. Novato, CA: Presidio, 2003.

Reischauer, Edwin. *Beyond Vietnam: The United States and Asia*. New York: Random House, 1967.

Williams, Glenn M. *So Others Might Live*. Mukilteo, WA: WinePress, 1998.

Index

E

Echo 4, 11, 35–36, 40, 42, 193,
        219n4, 223
El Paso, TX, 32, 34
EMs (enlisted men), 68, 82, 94, 104,
        113, 165
enemy, 17, 31, 56, 59, 78, 101, 103–4,
        110, 114, 166, 171, 174
Ervin, Fred, 37, 194–95
Erwin, Frank, 10, 11
Europe, 7, 49, 78

F

FBI, 22, 69
Field Forces Vietnam, 78, 100
First Indochina War, 55
fléchette canisters, 59
Fort Bliss, 32
Fort Sam Houston, xvi, xviii–2, 31–32,
        34–36, 38, 45, 49, 51, 90,
        184, 186, 192–95, 197, 206,
        223–24
fragging, 113–14
Franklin, Jim, 16
French Indochina, 55
friendship, 38–39, 67, 133, 141, 190
FSB, 62, 65, 138–39, 164
    Crook, 56
    Thunder(s) I, II, and III, 56, 59,
        62, 65
    Washington, 137–38

G

Gentle Thursday (Austin, TX), 12, 13
Gerding, Bert, 21
German House (Austin, TX), 8, 18,
        20, 187
GIs, xiii–xiv, 52, 55, 163
graduation, xvi–xvii, 4, 10, 17, 116
Graves Registration, 81, 89, 224
grunt, 54, 69, 90, 139, 165–66

H

Hacksaw Ridge, 28
Hailey, Jack, ix, 127, 145–50, 151
hazing, 3–5, 37
headquarters, xiii, 42, 53, 55, 96, 137,
        153, 161, 170–71
heat, 40–41, 51–52, 67, 99, 131,
        166–67, 174, 198, 202
helicopters, xiii, 53–54, 143–44, 103,
        153, 160, 163–65, 170–73,
        176, 178, 181
    Chinook helicopters, 67
    choppers, 62–63, 67, 121, 144, 154,
        161, 163–65, 171–72, 174–75,
        177, 192
    Huey, xiii–xiv, 103, 155, 160,
        164, 173
    Hughes OH-6A, 171
hero, 34, 108, 223
heroism, 28, 178, 183, 185
hoist, xiii, 172–75
    hot, 167, 170
Holiday, Mark "Doc," 170, 175, 223,
        178, 198, 228
Hong Kong, 117–20, 185
hooch. See barracks
Hoover, J. Edgar, 22
hospitals, 58, 91, 64, 119, 120–21, 139,
        183, 185, 192
    evacuation, 120, 161, 181, 183
    surgical, 58, 93, 198
Houston, TX, 19, 29–32, 116, 186, 211
Humphrey, Vice President Hubert, 14
Hurricane (newspaper), 78, 100,
        105–6

I

intensive care, 57, 107, 120, 121
Iron Triangle, 55, 56
IV (intravenous solution), 46–47, 55,
        143, 161